SIMPLY
OFFICE 2010

by Kate Shoup

WILEY

First published under the title Office 2010 Simplified, ISBN 978-0-470-57194-1 by Wiley Publishing, Inc. 10475 Crosspoint Boulevard, Indianapolis, IN 46256

Copyright © 2010 by Wiley Publishing, Inc., Indianapolis, Indiana

This edition first published 2010.

Copyright © 2010 for the EMEA adaptation: John Wiley & Sons, Ltd.

Registered office
John Wiley & Sons Ltd, The Atrium, Southern Gate, Chichester, West Sussex, PO19 8SQ, United Kingdom

For details of our global editorial offices, for customer services and for information about how to apply for permission to reuse the copyright material in this book please see our website at www.wiley.com.

All prices correct at time of going to press. Please check appropriate website for current details.

All website information was correct at the time of going to press. Websites do constantly update their privacy settings and policies. Please check the relevant website homepage to find their current policies.

ISBN: 978-0-470-71129-3

A catalogue record for this book is available from the British Library.

Printed in Italy by Printer Trento

Publisher's Acknowledgements

Editorial and Production

VP Consumer and Technology Publishing Director: Michelle Leete

Associate Director – Book Content Management: Martin Tribe

Associate Publisher: Chris Webb

Executive Commissioning Editor: Birgit Gruber

Publishing Assistant: Ellie Scott

Production Manager: Amie Jackowski Tibble

Project Editor: Juliet Booker

Development Editor: Shena Deuchars

Marketing:

Senior Marketing Manager: Louise Breinholt

Marketing Executive: Chloe Tunnicliffe

Composition Services:

Layout: Andrea Hornberger

Indexer: Potomac Indexing, LLC

Series Designer: Patrick Cunningham

About the Author

Freelance writer/editor **Kate Shoup** has authored 20 books and edited scores more. Recent titles include *Windows 7 Digital Classroom, Teach Yourself VISUALLY Outlook 2007, Office 2007: Top 100 Simplified Tips & Tricks and Internet Visual Quick Tips.* When not working, Kate loves to ski (she was once nationally ranked), read and ride her motorcycle – and she plays a mean game of nine-ball. Kate lives in Indianapolis with her daughter and their dog.

How to Use This Book

Do you look at the pictures in a book or magazine before anything else? Would you rather be shown instead of read about how to do something? Then this book is for you. Opening *Simply Office 2010* allows you to read less and learn more about the Windows operating system.

Who Needs This Book

This book is for a reader who has never used this particular technology or application. It is also for more computer literate individuals who want to expand their knowledge of the different features that Windows has to offer.

Using the Mouse

This book uses the following conventions to describe the actions you perform when using the mouse:

Click

Press your left mouse button once. You generally click your mouse on something to select something on the screen.

Double-click

Press your left mouse button twice. Double-clicking something on the computer screen generally opens whatever item you have double-clicked.

Right-click

Press your right mouse button. When you right-click anything on the computer screen, the program displays a shortcut menu containing commands specific to the selected item.

Click and Drag, and Release the Mouse

Move your mouse pointer and hover it over an item on the screen. Press and hold down the left mouse button. Now, move the mouse to where you want to place the item and then release the button. You use this method to move an item from one area of the computer screen to another.

The Conventions in This Book

A number of typographic and layout styles have been used throughout Simply *Office 2010* to distinguish different types of information.

Bold

Bold type represents the names of commands and options that you interact with. Bold type also indicates text and numbers that you must type into a dialog box or window.

Italics

Italic words introduce a new term and are followed by a definition.

Numbered Steps

You must perform the instructions in numbered steps in order to successfully complete a section and achieve the final results.

Bulleted Steps

These steps point out various optional features. You do not have to perform these steps; they simply give additional information about a feature. Steps without bullets tell you what the program does in response to your following a numbered step. For example, if you click a menu command, a dialog box may appear or a window may open. The step text may also tell you what the final result is when you follow a set of numbered steps.

Notes

Notes give additional information. They may describe special conditions that may occur during an operation. They may warn you of a situation that you want to avoid — for example, the loss of data. A note may also cross reference a related area of the book. A cross reference may guide you to another chapter or another section within the current chapter.

Icons and buttons

Icons and buttons are graphical representations within the text. They show you exactly what you need to click to perform a step.

You can easily identify the tips or warnings in any section by looking for the Tip and Warning icons. Tips offer additional information, including tips, hints, and tricks. You can use the tip information to go beyond what you have learned in the steps. Warnings tell you about solutions to common problems and general pitfalls to avoid.

Table of Contents

Chapter 4: Adding Text

Chapter 5: Formatting Text

Chapter 6: Adding Extra Touches

Chapter 7: Reviewing Documents

EXCEL   80

Chapter 8: Building Spreadsheets

Chapter 9: Worksheet Basics

Chapter 13: Assembling and Presenting a Slide Show

ACCESS   150

Chapter 14: Database Basics

Chapter 15: Adding, Finding and Querying Data

VI OUTLOOK 184

Chapter 16: Organising with Outlook

Chapter 17: E-mailing with Outlook

INDEX 208

CONTENTS

OFFICE FEATURES

In Office 2010, the applications share a common look and feel. You can find many of the same features in each program, such as the Ribbon, the Quick Access toolbar, various program window controls and the File tab. Many of the tasks you perform in Office, such as creating new files, opening existing files, working with text and data in files, saving files, printing files and executing commands, involve similar processes and features throughout the Office suite. In this part, you learn how to navigate the common Office features and perform basic Office tasks.

START AND EXIT OFFICE APPLICATIONS

Before you can begin working with a Microsoft Office application, also called a program, you must open the application.

There are a few ways to start an application. One is to launch it from the Start menu, as described in this task. Another is to double-click the program's shortcut icon on the desktop.

When you finish your work, you can close the program. If applicable, you can save your work before exiting a program completely.

Start an Office Application

1 Click **Start**.

2 Click **All Programs**.

Note: *The All Programs menu option changes to a Back menu option.*

3 Click **Microsoft Office**.

4 Click the name of the program that you want to open.

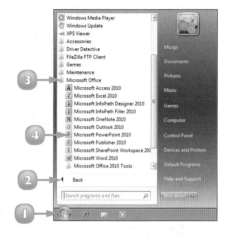

A *The program that you selected opens in a new window.*

Note: *See the next section to learn how to identify different areas of the program window.*

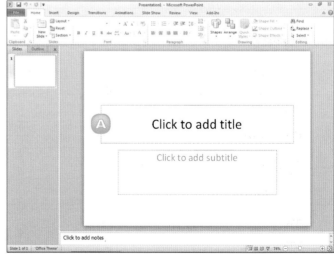

Exit an Office Application

① Click the **Close** button (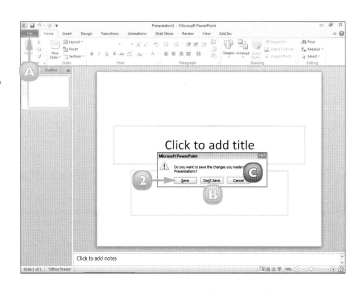).

> Ⓐ *You can also click the **File** tab and then click **Exit**.*

If you have not yet saved your work, the program prompts you to do so before exiting.

② Click **Save**.

The program window closes.

> Ⓑ *If you click **Don't Save**, the program closes without saving your data.*

> Ⓒ *If you click **Cancel**, the program window remains open.*

Create a Shortcut Icon for an Office Application

① Right-click a blank area of the desktop and click **New** and then **Shortcut**.

The Create Shortcut dialog box appears.

② Click **Browse**, navigate to the Office program, click the filename and click **OK**.

③ Click **Next**.

④ Type a name for the shortcut.

⑤ Click **Finish**.

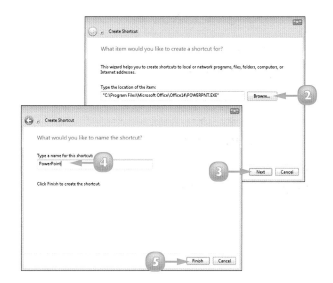

The new shortcut icon appears on the desktop.

NAVIGATE THE PROGRAM WINDOWS

All Office programs share a common appearance and many of the same features. These features include a Ribbon, which appears instead of the menus and toolbars found in previous versions of Microsoft Office; a Quick Launch toolbar, which features a customisable set of frequently used commands; and scroll bars, which you can use to navigate an open file in a program window. When you learn how to navigate one Office program, you can use the same skills to navigate the others. If you are new to Office, you should take a moment to familiarise yourself with the suite's various on-screen elements.

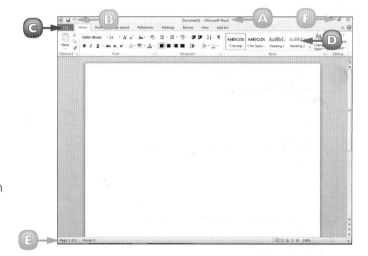

A Title Bar

Displays the name of the open file and the Office program.

B Quick Access Toolbar

Displays quick access buttons to the Save, Undo and Redo commands.

C File Tab Menu

Displays a menu of file commands, such as New and Open.

D Ribbon

Displays groups of related commands in tabs. Each tab offers buttons for performing common tasks.

E Status Bar

Displays information about the current worksheet or file.

F Program Window Controls

Displays buttons to minimise the program window, restore the window to full size and close the window.

A Formula Bar

This appears only in Excel. Use this bar to type and edit formulas and perform calculations on your worksheet data.

B Work Area

The area where you add and work with data in a program. Depending on the Office program, the work area may be a document, a worksheet or a slide.

C Document Window Controls

Use these buttons to minimise or restore the current document within the program window.

D Zoom Controls

Use this feature to zoom your view of a document.

E Scroll Bars

Use the vertical and horizontal scroll bars to scroll through the item shown in the work area.

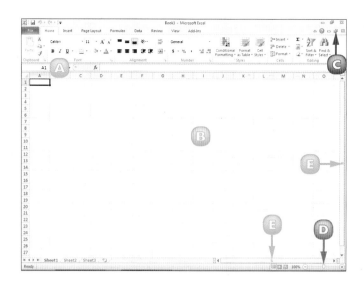

WORK WITH THE RIBBON

Instead of the menus and toolbars found in earlier versions of Office, Office 2010 features the Ribbon, which offers an intuitive way to locate and execute commands.

The Ribbon is grouped into tabs, each containing groups of related commands. For example, the Home tab in Microsoft Word contains commands for changing the font, setting text alignment, indenting text and so on. Some tabs appear only when needed, such as when you are working with a table or picture in a document.

The Ribbon is maximised by default, but you can minimise it to view more of your program window.

Use the Ribbon

1 Click a tab.

The tab organises related tasks and commands into logical groups.

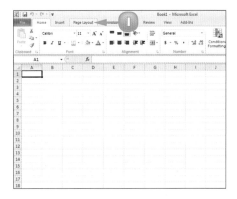

2 Click a button to activate a command or feature.

A *Buttons with arrows display additional commands.*

B *With some groups of commands, you can click the corner group button (⬜) to display a dialog box of additional settings.*

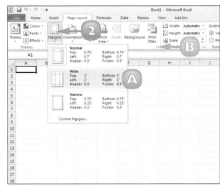

When you position the mouse pointer over Live Preview options on the Ribbon, you see the results in the document before applying the command.

Minimise the Ribbon

1 Double-click a tab name.

The Ribbon is minimised.

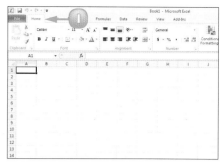

2 Double-click the tab name again to maximise the Ribbon.

Keep the Ribbon Minimised

1 Right-click a tab on the Ribbon.

2 Click **Minimize the Ribbon**.

The program's Ribbon is minimised at the top of the screen.

To use a Ribbon while it is minimised, simply click the tab containing the tools that you want to access.

CUSTOMISE THE QUICK ACCESS TOOLBAR

The Quick Access toolbar, which appears on-screen regardless of what tab is currently shown in the Ribbon, offers quick access to the Save, Undo and Redo commands.

You can customise this toolbar to include other commands, such as the Quick Print command or another command you use often. Alternatively, you might customise the toolbar to omit commands that appear by default.

By default, the Quick Access toolbar appears in the top left corner of the program window, above the Ribbon. You can choose to display the toolbar below the Ribbon instead.

1 Click the **Customize Quick Access Toolbar** button (⬇).

2 Click **More Commands**.

Ⓐ *You can click any of the common commands to add them to the toolbar.*

Ⓑ *You can click* **Show Below the Ribbon** *if you want to display the toolbar below the Ribbon.*

The Options dialog box opens with the options to customise the Quick Access Toolbar shown.

3 Click the **Choose commands from** ▾.

4 Click a command group.

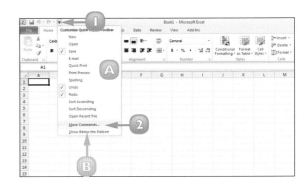

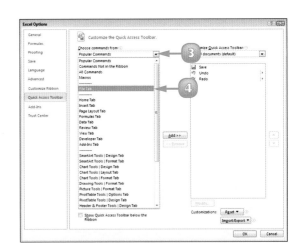

5 Click the command that you want to add to the toolbar.

6 Click the **Add** button.

 C *Office adds the command.*

You can repeat Steps **3** to **6** to move additional buttons to the toolbar.

7 Click **OK**.

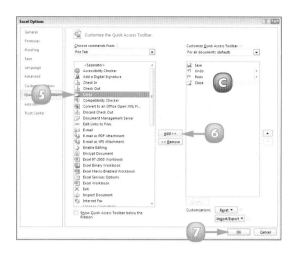

D *The new command appears on the Quick Access toolbar.*

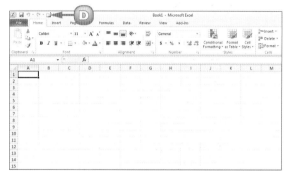

 *To remove a button from the Quick Access toolbar, open the Options dialog box, click the command name in the list box on the right, click the **Remove** button and click **OK**. The button no longer appears on the toolbar.*

 *You can add commands to the toolbar directly from the Ribbon. Simply click the tab containing the command that you want to add, right-click the command and then click **Add to Quick Access Toolbar**. The command is immediately added as a button on the toolbar.*

GET HELP WITH OFFICE

You can use Office Help to assist you when you run into a problem or need more information about how to complete a particular task.

The Help window offers tools that enable you to search for topics that you want to learn more about. For example, if you want to learn how to print an Office document, you can type Print in the Help window to locate articles on that topic. Alternatively, you can browse for articles by category. If you are connected to the Internet, you can access Microsoft's online help files for even more comprehensive information.

1 Click the **Help** button (🔘).

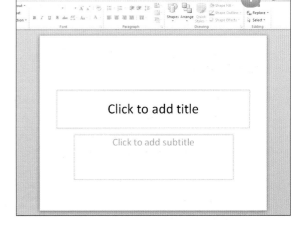

The Help window opens.

2 Type a word or phrase that you want to learn more about.

3 Click the **Search** button.

You can also press Enter to start the search.

Note: *You must be connected to the Internet to access Microsoft's online help files.*

The results window displays a list of possible matches.

④ Click a link to learn more about a topic.

The Help window displays the article, enabling you to read more about the topic.

Ⓐ You can use the **Back** and **Forward** buttons (◄ and ►) to move back and forth between help topics.

Ⓑ You can click the **Print** button (🖨) to print the information.

⑤ Click ☒ to close the window.

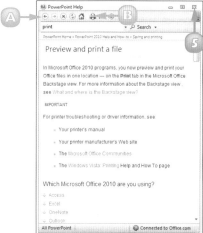

You can access the help files that are installed with Office if you are offline. However, the online resources offer you more help topics, as well as links to demos and other help tools.

To display a table of contents for the help files for the Office program that you are using, click the **Home** button (🏠) on the Help window's toolbar. Click a help category to display subtopics of help information. Click an article to view more about a topic. Many articles include links to related articles.

CREATE A NEW FILE

To work with data in Office 2010, you must create a file in which to store it. If the file you want to create is a Word document, an Excel workbook, an Access database, a PowerPoint presentation or a Publisher publication, you create a new file using the Getting Started screen. You are given the option of creating a blank file or basing the file on an existing template. To create a new item in Outlook, whether it is an e-mail message, a calendar appointment, a contact or a task item, you use the Ribbon.

Create a New Word, Excel, PowerPoint, Access or Publisher File

1 Click the **File** tab.

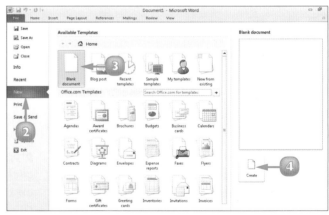

2 Click **New**.

The New screen appears.

3 Click the type of file that you want to create.

4 Click **Create**.

The new file opens.

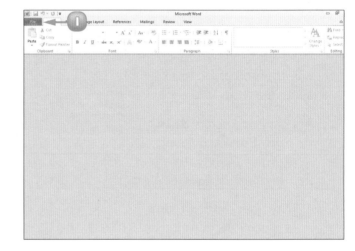

Note: *Another way to create a new file is to press* Ctrl+N. *Office creates a new file using the default settings.*

Create a New Outlook Item

 In the lower left corner of the Outlook window, click the type of item you want to create – Mail, Calendar, Contact or Task.

 Click the **New type** button, where *type* is the type of item. For example, if you are creating a Mail item, the button is labelled "New E-mail". If you are creating a Calendar item, the button is labelled "New Appointment", "New Meeting" and so on.

The new item opens.

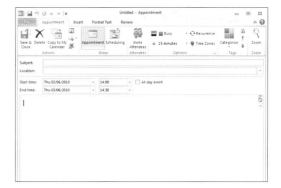

☑ **To create a new file from a template, simply click the desired template in the New screen.**

☑ **If you are connected to the Internet, you can access more Office templates. Simply click a template category under Office.com Templates in the New screen to display a list of available templates in the selected category; double-click one to download the template and apply it to a new file.**

15

SAVE A FILE

If you want to be able to refer to the data in a file at some later time, you must save the file. You should also frequently save any file you are working on to save losing data if a power failure or computer crash occurs.

When you save a file, you can give it a unique filename and store it in the folder or drive of your choice. You can also change the file type. You can then open the saved file at a later time. (See the next section for help opening Office files.)

1 Click the **File** tab.

A *For subsequent saves, you can click the **Save** button (🖫) on the Quick Access toolbar to quickly save the file.*

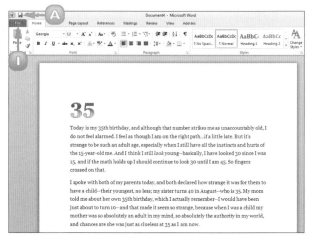

The document's Info screen appears.

2 Click **Save** or **Save As**.

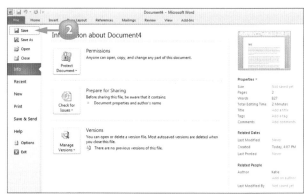

The Save As dialog box appears.

Note: *Another way to save a file is to press* **Ctrl** + **S**. *If this is the first time the file has been saved, Office launches the Save As dialog box.*

③ In the Navigation pane, click the library in which you want to save the file (here, Documents).

④ In the file list, navigate to the folder in which you want to save the file.

⑤ Type a name for the file in the **File name** field.

⑥ Click **Save**.

Ⓑ *The Office program saves the file and the new filename appears on the program window's title bar.*

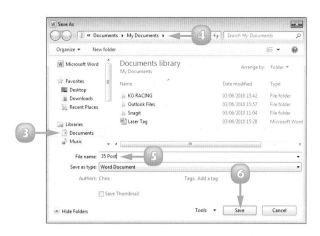

 *You can save files in a format compatible with previous versions of Office or with other programs. Click the **Save as Type** ▾ in the Save As dialog box and choose the desired format from the list that appears. Alternatively, with the file open, click the **File** tab, click **Share**, click **Change File Type** and choose the desired file type from the options that appear.*

 Each Office program saves to a default file type; for example, a Word document is saved in the DOCX file format.

OPEN A FILE

In addition to creating new files, you can open files that you have created and saved previously in order to continue adding data or to edit existing data.

Regardless of whether you store a file in a folder on your computer's hard drive or on a CD, you can easily access files using the Open dialog box. If you are not sure where you saved a file, you can use the Open dialog box's Search function to locate it.

When you are finished using a file, you should close it. Closing unnecessary files and programs frees up processing power on your computer.

① Click the **File** tab.

Ⓐ *If the file you want to open is listed under Recent Documents, click it.*

② Click **Open**.

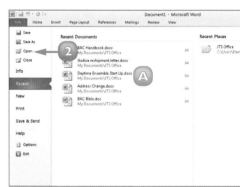

The Open dialog box appears.

Note: *Another way to launch the Open dialog box is to press* Ctrl + O.

③ In the Navigation pane, click the library in which the file you want to open has been saved (here, Documents).

④ In the file list, locate and click the folder in which the file you want to open has been saved.

⑤ Click **Open**.

⑥ Click the name of the file that you want to open.

⑦ Click **Open**.

The file opens in the program window.

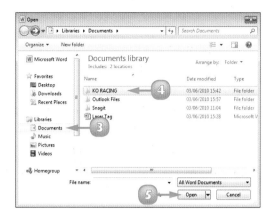

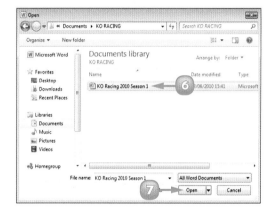

 To close a file, click the File tab and click Close in the screen that appears. Office closes the file, leaving the program window open. To close the open file and the program window, click the [X] button in the upper right corner of the program window.

 You can use the Search box in the upper right corner of the Open dialog box to locate files. Simply locate and open the folder in which you believe the file was saved and type the file's name in the Search box.

PRINT A FILE

If a printer is connected to your computer, you can print your Office files. For example, you might distribute printouts of a file as handouts in a meeting.

When you print a file, you have two options. You can send a file directly to the printer using the default settings or you can open the Office application's Print screen to change these settings. For example, you might opt to print just a portion of the file, print using a different printer, print multiple copies of a file, collate the printouts and so on. (Printer settings vary slightly among Office programs.)

1 Click the **File** tab.

2 Click **Print**.

The Print screen appears.

Note: *Another way to open the Print screen is to press* Ctrl + P .

A *You can specify the number of copies to print using the* **Copies** *spin box.*

B *You can choose a printer from the* **Printer** *drop-down list.*

C *You can choose to print a selection from the file or specific pages using the Settings list.*

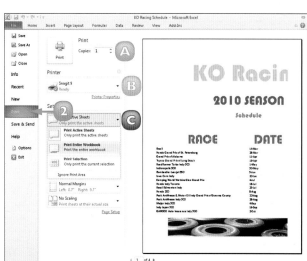

You can access additional print options under Settings.

 *View a preview of the printed file here.*

3 Click **Print**.

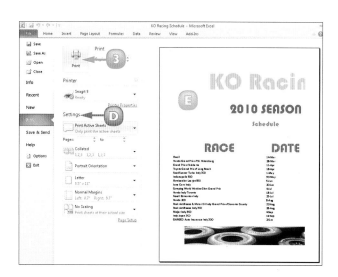

The Office program sends the file to the printer for printing.

 If you do not need to change any of the print settings, you can simply click the Quick Print button (🖶) on the Quick Access toolbar. If the Quick Print button does not appear on your Quick Access toolbar, you can add it (see Chapter 1).

You can add a Print Preview button to the Quick Access toolbar; clicking that button opens the Print screen.

SELECT DATA

Before you can perform different operations on data, such as deleting it, changing its font or alignment, applying a border around it, formatting it as a list or copying and pasting it elsewhere in a file or into a different file altogether, you must select the data. Selected data appears highlighted.

Depending on what program you are using, Office offers several different techniques for selecting data. For example, in Word, PowerPoint and Publisher, you can use your mouse or your keyboard to select a single character, a word, a sentence, a paragraph or all the data in the file.

Click and Drag to Select Data

1. Click to one side of the word or character that you want to select.

2. Drag the cursor across the text that you want to select.

   Word selects any characters that you drag across. You can use this technique to select characters, words, sentences and paragraphs.

   To deselect selected text, simply click anywhere outside the text or press any arrow key on your keyboard.

Note: *This technique also works for selecting images in your Office files. You can also select an image simply by clicking it.*

Select Text with a Mouse

 Double-click the word that you want to select.

You can triple-click a paragraph to select it.

Note: *To select data in Excel, click the cell that contains the data. To select a range of cells, click in the upper left corner of the range and drag down and to the right. To select cells that are not part of a continuous series, press* Ctrl *as you click each cell.*

Select Text from the Margin

Note: *This technique works only in Word.*

 Click in the left margin.

Word selects the entire line of text next to where you clicked.

You can double-click inside the left margin to select a paragraph.

You can triple-click inside the left margin to select all the text in the document.

REUNION

Last night I enjoyed a lovely dinner with some very old friends--people I hadn't seen in almost a decade, since before Heidi was born, let alone conceived. It was wonderful to catch up.

They live in Boston, which I am visiting on business. For one ill-fated semester in college, I lived here, attending Boston College and skiing for the ski team there. It was a disaster--everyone hated me (or at least I thought they did). My only refuge was at the home of these friends, Pepper and Stephanie, who took me in far more often than they probably would have liked. The house was plenty full without me. Pepper's mother had been recently divorced, and she had moved in with Pepper and Stephanie and their toddler daughter, Laura, as had two of Pepper's younger brothers, one of whom was about my age. But they never made me feel anything less than completely welcome. They were my family during a time when I desperately needed one.

REUNION

Last night I enjoyed a lovely dinner with some very old friends--people I hadn't seen in almost a decade, since before Heidi was born, let alone conceived. It was wonderful to catch up.

They live in Boston, which I am visiting on business. For one ill-fated semester in college, I lived here, attending Boston College and skiing for the ski team there. It was a disaster--everyone hated me (or at least I thought they did). My only refuge was at the home of these friends, Pepper and Stephanie, who took me in far more often than they probably would have liked. The house was plenty full without me. Pepper's mother had been recently divorced, and she had moved in with Pepper and Stephanie and their toddler daughter, Laura, as had two of Pepper's younger brothers, one of whom was about my age. But they never made me feel anything less than completely welcome. They were my family during a time when I desperately needed one.

You can also use keyboard shortcuts to select text in a file. To select a single word, press Ctrl + Shift + ← *or* Ctrl + Shift + →. *To select a paragraph from the cursor down or up, press* Ctrl + Shift + ↓ *or* Ctrl + Shift + ↑. *To select all of the text from the cursor onward, press* Ctrl + Shift + End. *To select all of the text above the current cursor location, press* Ctrl + Shift + Home. *To select all the text in the file, press* Ctrl + A.

CUT, COPY AND PASTE DATA

You can use the Cut, Copy and Paste commands to move or copy data. For example, you might cut or copy a picture from a Word document and paste it elsewhere in the same Word document, in another Word document or in a PowerPoint slide or a Publisher file.

When you cut data, it is removed from its original location; when you copy data, Office makes a duplicate of the selected data, leaving it in its original location. In addition to using the Cut, Copy and Paste commands to move and copy data, you can also use drag and drop.

Drag and Drop Data

① Select the data that you want to cut or copy.

② Click and drag the data to a new location.

The ⟨ changes to ⟨⟨.

To copy the data as you drag it, you can press and hold **Ctrl**.

③ Release the mouse to drop the data in place.

The data appears in the new location.

REUNION

Last night I enjoyed a lovely dinner with some very old friends--people I hadn't seen in almost a decade, since before Heidi was born, let alone conceived. It was wonderful to catch up.

They live in Boston, which I am visiting on business. For one ill-fated semester in college, I lived here, attending Boston College and skiing for the ski team there. It was a disaster--everyone hated me (or at least I thought they did). My only refuge was at the home of these friends, Pepper and Stephanie, who took me in far more often than they probably would have liked. The house was plenty full without me. Pepper's mother had been recently divorced, and she had moved in with Pepper and Stephanie and their toddler daughter, Laura, as had two of Pepper's younger brothers, one of whom was about my age. But they never made me feel anything less than completely welcome. They were my family during a time when I desperately needed one.

REUNION

Last night I enjoyed a lovely dinner with some very old friends--people I hadn't seen in almost a decade, since before Heidi was born, let alone conceived. It was wonderful to catch up.

They live in Boston, which I am visiting on business. For one ill-fated semester in college, I lived here, attending Boston College and skiing for the ski team there. It was a disaster--everyone hated me (or at least I thought they did). My only refuge was at the home of these friends, Pepper and Stephanie, who took me in far more often than they probably would have liked. Pepper's mother had been recently divorced, and she had moved in with Pepper and Stephanie and their toddler daughter, Laura, as had two of Pepper's younger brothers, one of whom was about my age. The house was plenty full without me. But they never made me feel anything less than completely welcome. They were my fam (Ctrl) ▾ g a time when I desperately needed one.

Cut and Copy Data

1 Select the data that you want to cut or copy.

2 Click the **Home** tab.

3 Click the **Cut** button () to move data or the **Copy** button () to copy data.

Note: *You can also press* Ctrl + X *to cut data or* Ctrl + C *to copy data.*

The data is stored in the Windows Clipboard.

4 Click the point where you want to insert the cut or copied data.

You can also open another file into which you can paste the data.

5 On the Home tab, click the **Paste** button.

Note: *You can also press* Ctrl + V *to paste data.*

A *The data appears in the new location.*

Note: *You can click the Paste Options smart tag () that appears when you paste, cut, or copy data to view various paste-related options.*

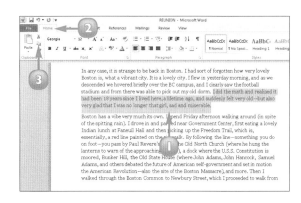

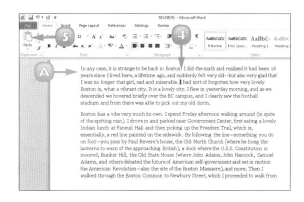

> ✓ **The Office Clipboard holds up to 24 items. You can paste them in whatever order you choose or you can paste them all at the same time. To display the task pane, click the corner group button () in the Clipboard group on the Ribbon's Home tab.**

> ✓ **You can display different views of a file or view multiple files at once. Open two or more files. Click the View tab and click Arrange All. Click the View Side by Side button () to see the open files side by side. Click the Synchronous Scrolling button () to scroll both files at the same time.**

INSERT A PICTURE OR CLIP ART

You can add interest to your Office files by inserting clip art or other images into them. Clip art is simply artwork or other types of media. Word, Excel, PowerPoint, Publisher and Outlook install with the Office clip art collection.

After you insert an image, you can resize, reposition, rotate and flip it. You can also perform other types of edits on the image, such as cropping, image correction, colour correction and more. Office 2010 also includes several tools, sometimes called *filters*, for applying artistic effects to images you insert in files.

1 Click the area where you want to add an image.

Note: *You can move the image to a different location after inserting it onto the page.*

2 Click the **Insert** tab.

3 In the Illustrations group, click **Picture**.

Alternatively, you can click **Clip Art** to open the Clip Art task pane.

The Insert Picture dialog box appears.

4 Navigate to the folder or drive containing the image file that you want to use.

A *To browse for a particular file type, you can click the ☐ and choose a file format.*

To remove a picture or clip art that you no longer want, you can click the picture and press Delete**.**

26

5 Click the file you want to add.

6 Click **Insert**.

Note: *Image files, also called objects, come in a variety of file formats, including GIF, JPEG and PNG.*

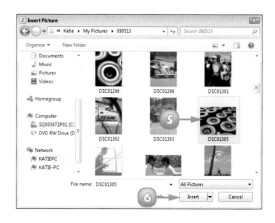

The picture is added to the file and the Picture tools appear on the Format tab.

You may need to resize or reposition the picture to fit the space.

Note: *See the "Resize and Move Objects" section to learn more.*

Search for Clip Art

1 In the Clip Art task pane, type a keyword or phrase in the **Search for** field.

A *To specify what type of item you need — illustration, photograph, video or audio — click the* **Results should be** *and click the type of item.*

B *You can search for clip art on the Office Web site by clicking to select the* **Include Office. com content** *check box.*

2 Click **Go**.

The Clip Art task pane displays any matches for the keyword or phrase that you typed.

3 To insert a clip art image, click it.

 You can compress images that you add to an Office file to make the file smaller. Click the image, click the Format tab on the Ribbon, and click the Compress Pictures button ( ) in the Adjust group. Adjust settings as needed in the Compress Pictures dialog box and click OK.

RESIZE AND MOVE OBJECTS

Clip art and other types of images, such as smart art and word art, are called **objects**. When you insert an object, such as an image, into an Office file, you may find that you need to make it larger or smaller in order to achieve the desired effect. Fortunately, doing so is easy. When you select an object in an Office file, handles appear around that object; you can use these handles to make the object larger or smaller. You can also move objects that you place in a file.

Resize an Object

1 Click the object that you want to resize.

2 Click a selection handle.

3 Drag inward or outward to resize the object.

Note: *To maintain an object's height-to-width ratio when resizing, drag one of the corner handles.*

When you release the mouse button, the object is resized.

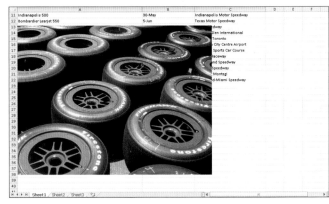

Move an Object

① Click the object that you want to move.

② Drag the object to a new location on the worksheet.

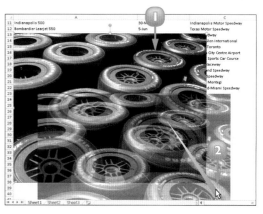

When you release the mouse button, the object moves to the new location.

Note: *You can also move an object by cutting it from its current location and pasting it in the desired spot. For help, refer to the section "Cut, Copy and Paste Data" in Chapter 2.*

Wrap Text Around an Object

① Click the object.

② Click the **Text Wrapping** button in the Format tab.

③ Choose a wrap style.

ROTATE AND FLIP OBJECTS

After you insert an object such as a piece of clip art or a photo from your hard drive into a Word document, an Excel worksheet, a PowerPoint slide or a Publisher brochure, you may find that the object appears upside down or inverted. To rectify this, you can rotate or flip the object. For example, you might flip a clip art image to face another direction or rotate an arrow object to point elsewhere on the page. Alternatively, you might rotate or flip an object that you place in an Office 2010 file simply to change the appearance of that object.

Rotate an Object

1 Click the object that you want to rotate.

   A *A rotation handle appears on the selected object.*

2 Click and drag the handle to rotate the object.

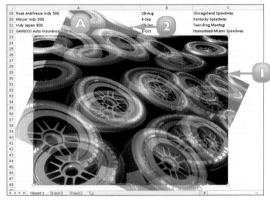

   B *When you release the mouse, the object rotates.*

Note: *You can also use the* **Rotate** *button (🔲) on the Format tab on the Ribbon to rotate an object 90 degrees left or right.*

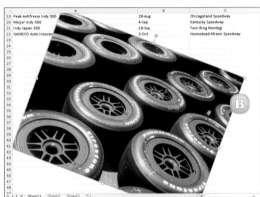

30

Flip an Object

 Click the object that you want to flip.

The Format tab opens and displays the Picture tools.

 Click the **Rotate** button ().

 Click **Flip Vertical** or **Flip Horizontal**.

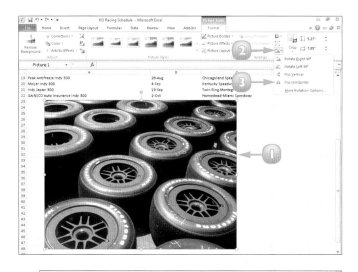

The object flips.

To constrain the rotation to 15-degree increments, press and hold Shift while using the rotation handle to rotate the object. Rotate the object in 90-degree increments by clicking the Rotate button () on the Format tab and choosing Rotate Right 90° or Rotate Left 90°.

CROP A PICTURE

In addition to resizing an Office object, such as a clip art image or a photo you have stored on your computer's hard drive, you can use the Crop tool to crop it. When you crop an object, you remove vertical and/or horizontal edges from the object. For example, you might use the Crop tool to create a better fit, to omit a portion of the image or to focus the viewer on an important area of the image. The Crop tool is located on the Format tab on the Ribbon, which appears when you click the object you want to crop.

① Click the image that you want to edit.

   Ⓐ The Format tab opens and displays the Picture tools.

② Click the **Crop** button.

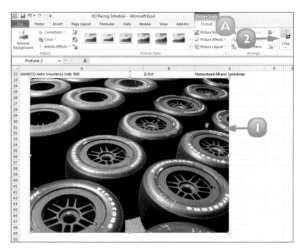

   Ⓑ Crop handles surround the image.

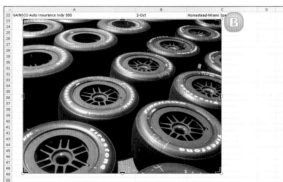

3 Click and drag a crop handle to crop out an area of the image.

When you release the mouse button, the image is cropped.

4 Click outside the image to finalise the crop operation.

Note: See the "Resize and Move Objects" section, earlier in this chapter, to learn how to resize an image.

Crop Objects into Predefined Shapes

1 Click the object you want to crop.

2 Click the **Format** tab.

3 Click the **Crop** ▾

4 Click **Crop to Shape** and choose the desired shape from the menu.

CHANGE A PICTURE

Suppose the image object you have inserted into your Office 2010 file is less than perfect. Perhaps it is slightly blurry, lacks contrast or the colour seems off. Fortunately, Office 2010 offers tools that enable you to make corrections to clip art and images even after they have been inserted into your file. For example, you can sharpen and soften images, as well as adjust their brightness and contrast. You can also adjust colours using the Office 2010 Color Saturation, Color Tone and Recolor tools.

Office 2010 includes several tools, sometimes referred to as **filters**, for applying artistic effects to images and clip art. For example, you can apply an artistic effect to make an image appear as though it was rendered in marker pen, pencil, chalk or paint.

Click the picture that you want to edit. The Format tab appears on the Ribbon with the Picture tools shown.

Make Image Corrections

1 In the Adjust group, click the **Corrections** button.

   A *Office highlights the image's current correction settings.*

   B *As you drag over each setting in the menu, the picture displays what the setting looks like when you apply it.*

2 Click a correction setting.

   The new setting is applied to the picture.

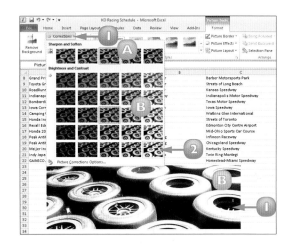

Make Colour Adjustments

1 In the Adjust group, click the **Color** button.

2 Click a colour setting.

   The new setting is applied to the picture.

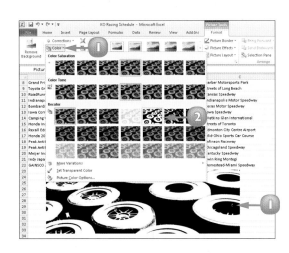

Apply Artistic Effects

 In the Adjust group, click the **Artistic Effects** button.

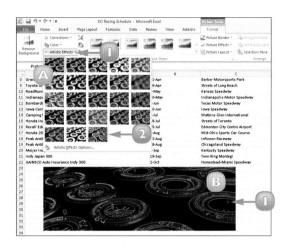

Ⓐ *Office highlights the image's current effect.*

Ⓑ *As you drag over each effect in the menu, the picture displays what the effect looks like.*

② Click an artistic effect.

The new setting is applied to the picture.

Apply a Picture Effect

① In the Picture Styles group, click the **Picture Effects** button.

② Click an effect category.

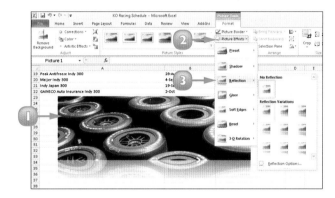

Note: *As you drag over each effect in the menu, the picture displays what the effect looks like when you apply it.*

③ Click an effect style.

The new setting is applied to the picture.

> ✓ ***As you drag over each setting in the menu, the picture displays what the setting looks like when you apply it.***

CONTENTS

WORD

You can use Word to tackle any project involving text, such as letters, faxes, memos, reports, manuscripts. Word's versatile formatting features enable you to enhance your text documents with ease, changing the font size and colour, altering the text alignment and more. You can also add elements such as tables, headers and footers, page numbers, a table of contents, even an index. Word offers a variety of editing tools to help you make your document look its best. In this part, you learn how to build and format Word documents and tap into Word's many tools to preview, proofread and print your documents.

CHANGE WORD'S VIEWS

Microsoft Word offers you several ways to control how you view your document. For example, the Zoom tool enables you to control the magnification of your document. You can change the zoom setting by using the Zoom slider or the Zoom buttons.

You can also choose from five different views: Print Layout, which displays margins, headers and footers; Outline, which shows the document's outline levels; Web Layout, which displays a Web page preview of your document; Full Screen Reading, which optimises your document for easier reading; and Draft, which omits certain elements such as headers and footers.

Use the Zoom Tool

1. Drag the **Zoom** slider on the Zoom bar.

   A. *You can also click a magnification button to zoom in or out.*

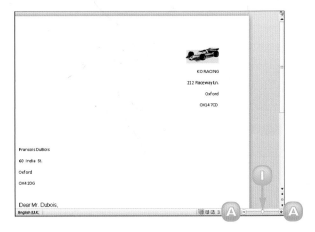

Word applies the magnification to the document.

Switch Layout Views

1. Click the **View** tab on the Ribbon.

2. Click a layout view button.

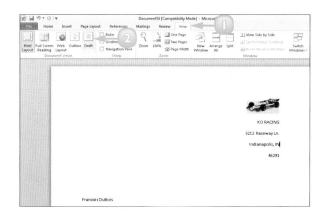

Word displays the new view.

A. *In this example, Draft view displays the text without graphics or other elements.*

B. *You can also switch views using the View buttons at the bottom of the program window.*

 Use the scroll bars to move up and down a document page. Alternatively, press the arrow keys on your keyboard to move up, down, left and right in the document. You can also press `Page up` and `Page down` to move to the preceding or next page in the document.

 If your document's structure incorporates headings, subheadings and body text, you can use Outline view to see and change the document structure. Switching to Outline view displays the Outlining tab, with buttons for changing heading styles and levels.

TYPE AND EDIT TEXT

When you launch Microsoft Word, a blank document appears, ready for you to start typing.

If you repeatedly type the same text in your documents, for example, your company name, you can add this text to Word's Quick Parts Gallery; then, the next time you need to add the text to a document, you can select it from the gallery instead of retyping it.

Type Text

1 Start typing your text.

Word automatically wraps the text to the next line for you.

A *The insertion point, or cursor, marks the location where text appears.*

2 Press **Enter** to start a new paragraph.

B *You can press **Tab** to quickly create an indent for a line of text.*

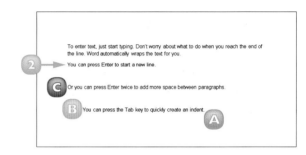

Edit Text

1 Click in the document where you want to fix a mistake.

A *Press **Backspace** to delete characters to the left of the cursor.*

B *Press **Delete** to delete characters to the right of the cursor.*

You can also delete selected text.

Note: *If you make a spelling mistake, Word either corrects the mistake or underlines it in red.*

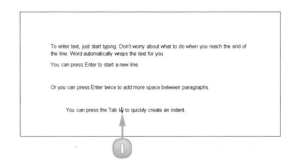

Add a Quick Parts Entry

1. Select the text that you want to add to the Quick Parts Gallery.

2. Click the **Insert** tab on the Ribbon and then the **Quick Parts** button.

3. Click **Save Selection to Quick Part Gallery**.

   The Create New Building Block dialog box appears.

4. Type a name for the entry or use the default name.

   You can also assign a gallery, a category and a description for the entry.

5. Click **OK**.

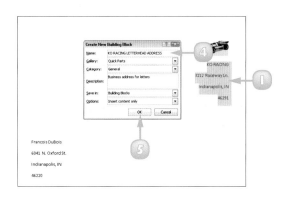

Insert a Quick Part Entry

1. Click in the text where you want to insert a Quick Part.

2. Click the **Insert** tab on the Ribbon and then the **Quick Parts** button.

3. Click the entry that you want to insert.

   Word inserts the entry into the document.

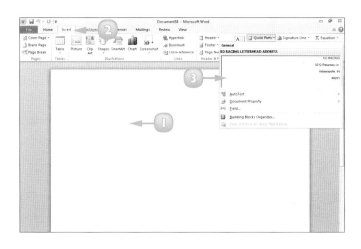

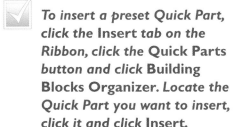
To insert a preset Quick Part, click the Insert tab on the Ribbon, click the Quick Parts button and click Building Blocks Organizer. Locate the Quick Part you want to insert, click it and click Insert.

By default, Word is set to Insert mode: when you start typing, any existing text moves over to accommodate the new text. You can press [Insert] to switch to Overtype mode, in which new text overwrites existing text.

INSERT SYMBOLS AND SPECIAL CHARACTERS

From time to time, you might need to insert a special symbol or character into your Word document, such as a mathematical symbol, that is not on your keyboard. You can use the Symbol palette to access a wide range of symbols, including mathematical and Greek symbols, architectural symbols and more. You can also use the Symbol dialog box to insert special characters such as em dashes, copyright symbols and so on.

Insert a Symbol

1 Click where you want to insert a symbol.

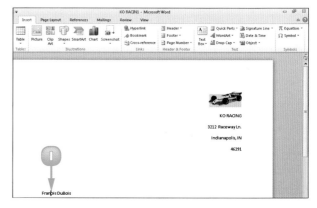

2 Click the **Insert** tab.

3 Click the **Symbol** button.

4 If the symbol you want to insert appears in the Symbol palette, click it. Otherwise, click **More Symbols**.

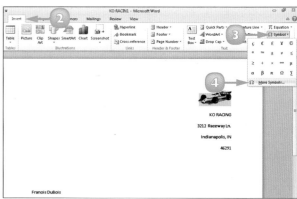

The Symbol dialog box appears.

⑤ Click the character that you want to insert.

Ⓐ *You can click the* **Font** ▾ *and click another font to change the symbols that appear in the Symbols tab.*

⑥ Click **Insert**.

Ⓑ *Word adds the character to the current cursor location in the document.*

The dialog box remains open so that you can add more characters to your text.

⑦ When finished, click **Close**.

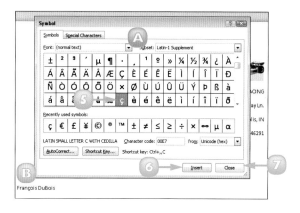

François DuBois

Insert a Special Character

① Click the **Symbol** button.

② Choose **More Symbols** to open the Symbol dialog box.

③ Click the **Special Characters** tab.

④ Locate and click the character you want to add and then click **Insert**.

⑤ Click **Close** to close the dialog box.

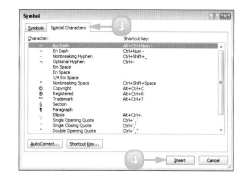

43

CHANGE THE FONT, SIZE AND COLOUR

By default, when you type text in a Word 2010 document, the program uses 11-point Calibri font. You can change the text font, size and colour to alter the appearance of text in a document. For example, you might change the font, size, and colour of your document's title text to emphasise it. You can also change the font that Word 2010 applies by default.

Change the Font

1. Select the text that you want to format.

2. Click the **Home** tab on the Ribbon.

3. Click the **Font** ⏷.

4. Click a font.

   Word applies the font to the text.

Change the Size

1. Select the text that you want to format.

2. Click the **Home** tab on the Ribbon.

3. Click the **Font Size** ⏷.

4. Click a size.

   Word applies the font size to the text, in this case, 48 points.

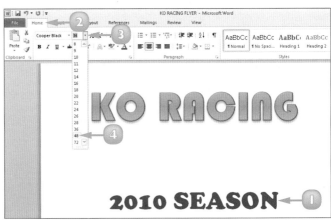

Note: If you click the **Grow Font** (A̅) and **Shrink Font** (A̅) buttons on the Home tab, Word increases or decreases the font size.

44

Change the Colour

① Select the text that you want to format.

② Click the **Home** tab on the Ribbon.

③ Click the 🔽 next to the **Font Color** button (🔺).

④ Click a colour.

Word applies the colour to the text.

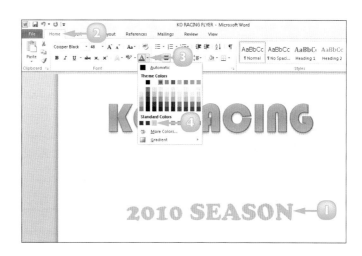

Use the Font Dialog Box

① Select the text that you want to format.

② Click the **Home** tab on the Ribbon.

③ Click the corner group button (⬜) in the Font group.

The Font dialog box appears.

④ Click the font, style, size, colour, underline style or effect that you want to apply.

⑤ Click **OK**.

Word applies the font change.

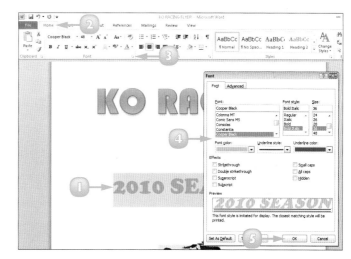

✓ *To change the default font and size, display the Font dialog box. Click the font options that you want to set as defaults. Click the Set As Default button. In the new dialog box, specify whether the change should apply to this document only or to all documents created with the current template.*

ALIGN TEXT

You can use Word's alignment commands to change how text and objects are positioned horizontally on a page. By default, Word left-aligns text and objects. You can also choose to centre text and objects on a page (using the Center command), align text and objects to the right side of the page (using the Right Align command) or justify text and objects so that they line up at both the left and right margins of the page (using the Justify command). You can change the alignment of all the text and objects in your document or change the alignment of individual paragraphs and objects.

① Select the text that you want to format.

② Click the **Home** tab on the Ribbon.

③ Click an alignment button.

Click the **Align Left** button (▤) to left-align text.

Click the **Center** button (▤) to centre text.

Click the **Align Right** button (▤) to right-align text.

Click the **Justify** button (▤) to justify text between the left and right margins.

Ⓐ *Word applies the alignment to the text.*

This example centres the text on the document page.

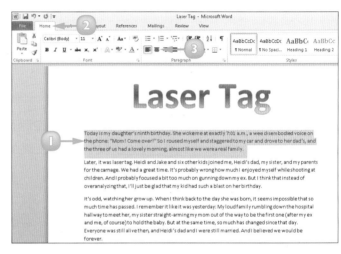

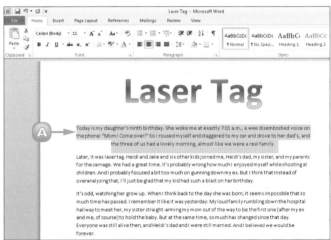

SET LINE SPACING

You can adjust the amount of spacing that appears between lines of text in your paragraphs. For example, you might set 2.5 spacing to allow for handwritten edits in your printed document or set 1.5 spacing to make paragraphs easier to read. By default, Word assigns 1.15 spacing for all new documents that you create.

You can also control how much space appears before and after each paragraph in your document. For example, you might opt to single-space the text within a paragraph but add space before and after the paragraph to set it apart from the paragraphs that precede and follow it.

① Select the text that you want to format.

② Click the **Home** tab on the Ribbon.

③ Click the **Line Spacing** button (▤).

④ Click a line spacing option.

Ⓐ *Word immediately applies the new spacing.*

This example applies 2.0 line spacing.

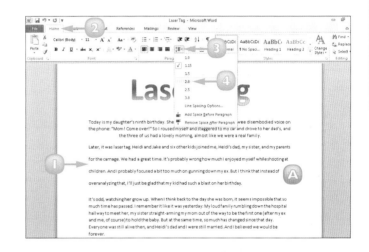

⑤ To control the spacing that surrounds a paragraph, click the corner group button (▣) in the Paragraph group.

The Paragraph dialog box opens.

⑥ Use the **Before** spin box to specify how much space should appear before the paragraph.

⑦ Use the **After** spin box to specify how much space should appear after the paragraph.

⑧ Click **OK**.

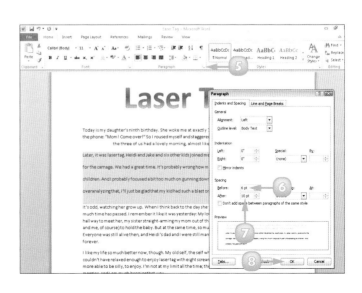

INDENT TEXT

You can use indents as another way to control the horizontal positioning of text in a document. Indents are simply margins that affect individual lines or paragraphs. You might use an indent to distinguish a particular paragraph on a page – for example, a long quote.

Word offers several tools for setting indents. For example, the Home tab on the Ribbon contains buttons for quickly increasing and decreasing indents by a predefined amount. You can make more precise changes to indent settings in the Paragraph dialog box. Finally, you can use the Word ruler to set indents.

Set Quick Indents

① Click anywhere in the paragraph you want to indent.

② Click the **Home** tab on the Ribbon.

③ Click an indent button.

You can click the **Decrease Indent** button (⊞) to decrease the indentation.

You can click the **Increase Indent** button (⊞) to increase the indentation.

Ⓐ *Word applies the indent change.*

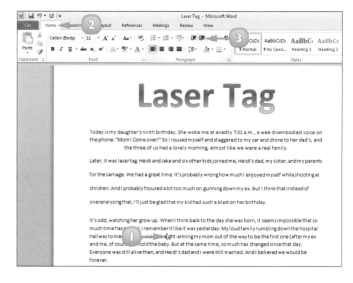

Set Precise Indents

1. Click anywhere in the paragraph you want to indent.

2. Click the **Home** tab on the Ribbon.

3. Click the corner group button (▣) in the Paragraph group.

   The Paragraph dialog box appears.

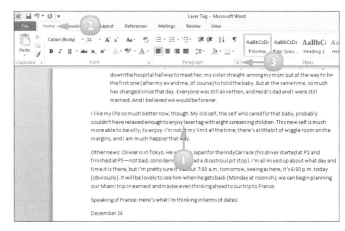

4. Type a specific indentation in the **Left** or **Right** indent text boxes.

   A *You can also click ⬍ to set an indent measurement.*

   B *To set a specific kind of indent, you can click the **Special** ▾ and then click an indent.*

   C *The Preview area shows a sample of the indent.*

5. Click **OK**.

   Word applies the indent to the text.

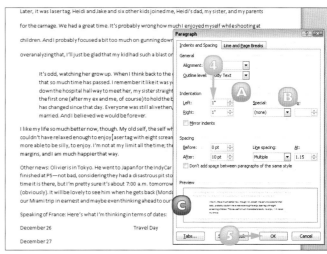

You can quickly set an indent using the Word ruler. To do so, simply drag the indent marker (▣) on the ruler to the desired location. If the ruler is not visible, position your mouse pointer over the top of the work area and pause; the ruler appears. (You can also click

the View tab and click Ruler to display the ruler). The ruler contains markers for changing the left indent, right indent, first-line indent and hanging indent. (To determine which marker is which, you can position your mouse pointer over each one; Word displays the marker's name.)

SET TABS

You can use tabs to create vertically aligned columns of text in your Word document. To insert a tab, simply press the key on your keyboard; the cursor moves to the next tab stop on the page.

By default, Word creates tab stops every 0.5 inches across the page and left-aligns the text on each tab stop. You can set your own tab stops using the ruler or the Tabs dialog box. You can also use the Tabs dialog box to change the tab alignment and specify an exact measurement between tab stops.

Set Quick Tabs

1. Position your mouse pointer over the top edge of the work area and pause to display the ruler.

   Ⓐ *You can also click the* **View** *tab and click* **Ruler** *to turn on the ruler.*

2. Click the **Tab marker** area to cycle through to the type of tab marker that you want to set.

   ▣ sets a left-aligned tab.

   ▣ sets a centre-aligned tab.

   ▣ sets a right-aligned tab.

   ▣ sets a decimal tab.

   ▣ sets a bar tab.

3. Click in the ruler where you want to insert the tab.

4. Click at the end of the text after which you want to add a tab.

5. Press **Tab**.

6. Type the text that should appear in the next column.

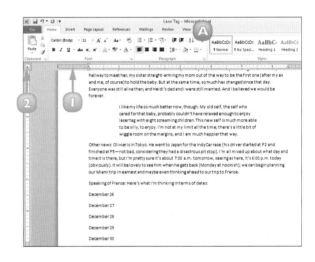

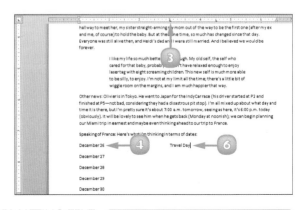

Set Precise Tabs

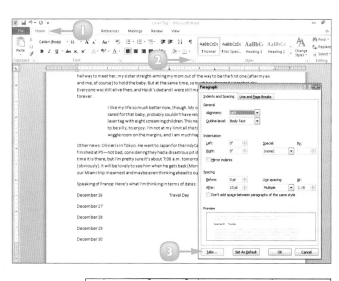

1 Click the **Home** tab on the Ribbon.

2 Click the corner group button (⬜) in the Paragraph group.

The Paragraph dialog box appears.

3 Click **Tabs** on the Indents and Spacing tab.

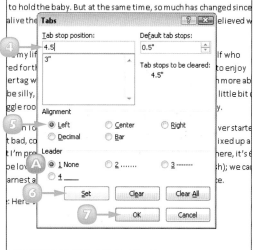

The Tabs dialog box appears.

4 Click in the **Tab stop position** text box and type a new tab stop measurement.

5 Click to select a tab alignment.

A *You can also select a tab leader character.*

6 Click **Set**.

Word saves the new tab stop.

7 Click **OK**.

Word exits the dialog box and you can use the new tab stops.

 To remove a tab stop from the ruler, drag it off the ruler. To remove a tab stop in the Tabs dialog box, select it and then click Clear. To clear every tab stop that you saved in the Tabs dialog box, click Clear All.

 You can use tab leaders to separate tab columns with dots, dashes or lines. Leaders help readers follow the information across tab columns.

SET MARGINS

By default, Word assigns a 1-inch margin all the way around the page in every new document that you create. You can change these margin settings, however. For example, you can set wider margins to fit more text on a page or set smaller margins to fit less text on a page. You can apply your changes to the current document only or set them as the new default setting, to be applied to all new Word documents you create.

Set Margins Using Page Layout Tools

① Click the **Page Layout** tab on the Ribbon.

② Click the **Margins** button.

③ Click a margin setting.

Word applies the new settings.

Set a Custom Margin

 Click the **Page Layout** tab on the Ribbon.

② Click the **Margins** button.

③ Click **Custom Margins**.

The Page Setup dialog box opens, with the Margins tab shown.

④ Type a specific margin in the **Top**, **Bottom**, **Left** and **Right** boxes.

 You can also click ⬦ to set a margin measurement.

⑤ Choose a page orientation.

⑥ Preview the margin settings in the Preview section.

⑦ Click the **Apply to** ▾ and specify whether the margins should apply to the whole document or from this point in the document forward.

⑧ Click **OK**.

Word immediately adjusts the margins in the document.

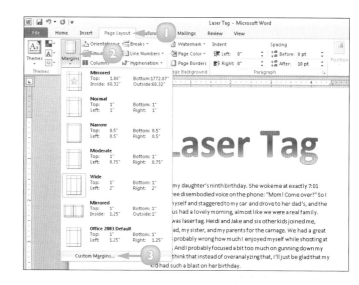

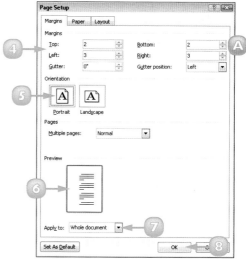

✓ **If you consistently use the same margin settings, you can choose those settings as the default for every new document that you create in Word. To do so, make the desired changes to the Margins tab of the Page Setup dialog box and then click Set As Default.**

🛑 **Some printers have a minimum margin in which nothing can be printed. For example, with many printers, anything less than 0.25 inches is outside the printable area. Be sure to test the margins or check your printer documentation for more information.**

COPY FORMATTING

Suppose you have applied a variety of formatting options to a paragraph to create a certain look – for example, you changed the font, the size, the colour and the alignment. If you want to re-create the same look elsewhere in the document, you do not have to repeat the same steps as when you applied the original formatting. Instead, you can use Word's Format Painter feature to "paint" the formatting to the other text in one swift action. With the Format Painter feature, copying formatting is as easy as clicking a button.

① Select the text that contains the formatting that you want to copy.

② Click the **Home** tab on the Ribbon.

③ Click the **Format Painter** button (▨).

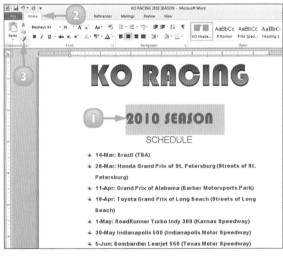

④ Click and drag over the text to which you want to apply the same formatting.

Word immediately copies the formatting to the new text.

Note: *To copy the same formatting multiple times, you can double-click the Format Painter button (▨).*

You can press Esc to cancel the Format Painter feature at any time.

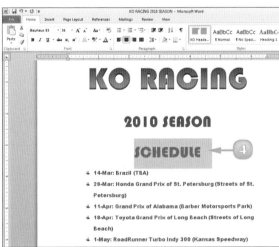

54

CLEAR FORMATTING

Sometimes, you may find that you have applied too much formatting to your text, making it difficult to read. Or perhaps you simply applied the wrong formatting to your text. In that case, instead of undoing all your formatting changes by hand, you can use Word's Clear Formatting command to remove any formatting you have applied to the document text. When you apply the Clear Formatting command, Word removes all formatting applied to the text and restores the default settings.

1. Select the text containing the formatting that you want to remove.

2. Click the **Home** tab on the Ribbon.

3. Click the **Clear Formatting** button (⌫).

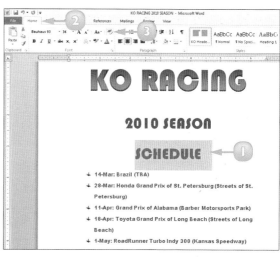

Word immediately removes the formatting and restores the default settings.

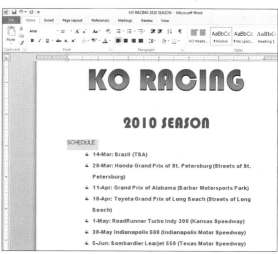

FORMAT WITH STYLES

Suppose you are writing a corporate report that requires specific formatting for every heading. Instead of assigning multiple formatting settings over and over again, you can create a style with the required formatting settings and apply it whenever you need it. A *style* is a set of text-formatting characteristics. These characteristics might include the text font, size, colour, alignment, spacing and more.

In addition to creating your own styles for use in your documents, you can apply any of Word's preset styles. These include styles for headings, normal text, quotes and more.

Create a New Quick Style

1. Format the text as desired and then select the text.

2. Click the **Home** tab on the Ribbon.

3. Click the **More** button (⬇) in the Styles group.

4. Click **Save Selection as a New Quick Style**.

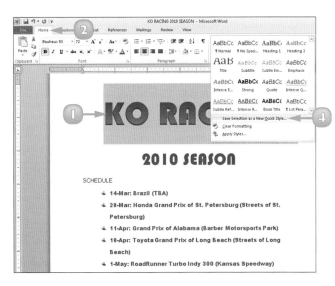

The Create New Style from Formatting dialog box appears.

5. Type a name for the style.

6. Click **OK**.

Word adds the style to the list of Quick Styles.

Apply a Quick Style

 Select the text that you want to format.

 Click the **Home** tab on the Ribbon.

 Click a style from the Styles list.

Note: *You can click the **More** button (⊞) to see the full palette of available styles.*

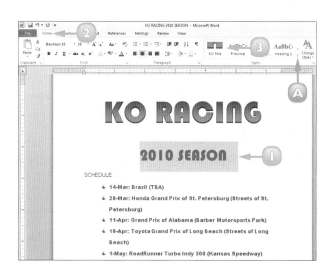

Word applies the style.

 To remove a style that you no longer need, from the Home tab, display the full Quick Styles palette, right-click the style that you want to remove and click the Remove from Quick Style Gallery command. Word immediately removes the style from the Quick Styles list.

 To customise an existing style, apply it to some text. Then, with the text selected, click the Home tab, click the Change Styles button and click the type of change that you want to make. For example, to switch fonts, click the Fonts option and then select another font.

APPLY A TEMPLATE

A *template* is a special file that stores styles and other Word formatting tools. When you apply a template to a Word document, the styles and tools in that template become available for your use with that document. Word comes with several templates preinstalled; in addition, you can create your own.

Of course, one way to apply a template to a document is to select it from the list of document types in the New screen that appears when you create a new Word document. Alternatively, you can attach a template to an existing document, as outlined here.

1. With the document to which you want to apply a template open in Word, click the **File** tab.

2. Click **Options**.

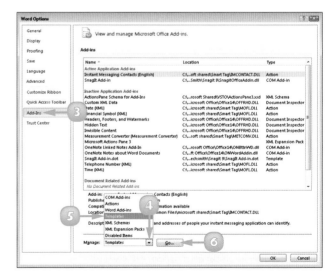

The Word Options window opens.

3. Click **Add-Ins**.

4. Click the **Manage** ▾.

5. Click **Templates**.

6. Click **Go**.

The Templates and Add-ins dialog box opens.

⑦ Click to select the **Automatically update document styles** check box.

⑧ Click **Attach**.

The Attach Template dialog box opens.

⑨ Locate and select the template you want to apply.

⑩ Click **Open**.

Word applies the template.

The styles used in the document are updated to reflect those appearing in the template.

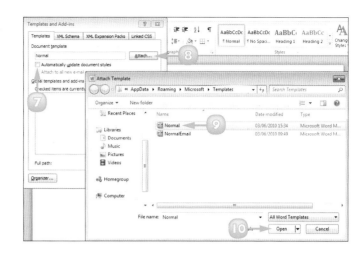

*The easiest way to create a template is to base it on an existing Word document. With the document on which you want to base your template open in Word, click the **File** tab and click **Save As**. The Save As dialog box opens; locate and select the folder in which you want to save the template, type a name for the template in the **File Name** field, click the Save as Type ▾, choose **Word Template** and click **Save**. Word saves the template in the folder you chose.*

CREATE COLUMNS

You can create columns in Word to present your text in a format similar to a newspaper or magazine. For example, if you are creating a brochure or newsletter, you can use columns to make text flow from one block to the next.

If you simply want to create a document with two or three columns, you can use one of Word's preset column settings. Alternatively, you can create custom columns, choosing the number of columns you want to create in your document, indicating the width of each column, specifying whether a line should appear between them and more.

Create Quick Columns

1. Select the text that you want to place into columns.

2. Click the **Page Layout** tab on the Ribbon.

3. Click the **Columns** button.

4. Click the number of columns that you want to assign.

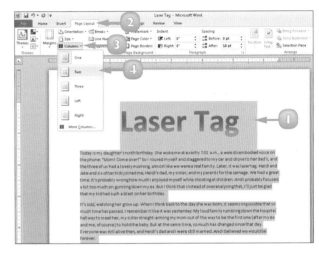

Word places the selected text in the number of columns that you specify.

Create Custom Columns

① Select the text that you want to place into columns.

② Click the **Page Layout** tab on the Ribbon.

③ Click the **Columns** button.

④ Click **More Columns**.

The Columns dialog box appears.

⑤ Click a preset for the type of column style that you want to apply.

Ⓐ You can specify the number of columns here.

Ⓑ You can set an exact column width and spacing here.

Ⓒ You can specify whether the columns apply to the selected text or the entire document.

Ⓓ You can include a vertical line separating the columns.

⑥ Click **OK**.

Word applies the column format to the selected text.

To add a column break, click where you want the break to occur and then press Ctrl + Shift + Enter. To remove a break, select it and press Delete. To return to a one-column format, click the Columns button on the Page Layout tab and then select the single-column format.

To wrap column text around a picture or other object, click the picture or object, click the Format tab, click the **Wrap Text** button and then click the type of wrapping that you want to apply.

INSERT A TABLE

You can use tables to present data in an organised fashion. For example, you might add a table to your document to display a list of items or a roster of classes. Tables contain columns and rows, which intersect to form *cells*. You can insert all types of data in cells, including text and graphics. When you click in a table, two new tabs appear on the Ribbon: Design and Layout. You can use the table styles found in the Design tab to add instant formatting to your Word tables.

If Excel is installed on your computer, you can insert an Excel spreadsheet into your Word document. The Ribbon in Word changes to display various Excel tools and features that you use to work with data you add to the spreadsheet.

Insert a Table

1. Click in the document where you want to insert a table.

2. Click the **Insert** tab on the Ribbon.

3. Click the **Table** button.

4. Drag across the number of columns and rows that you want to set for your table.

   A. *Word previews the table as you drag over the cells.*

5. Click inside a cell and type your data.

Insert a Quick Table

1. Click in the document where you want to insert a table.

2. Click the **Insert** tab on the Ribbon.

3. Click the **Table** button.

4. Click **Quick Tables**.

5. Click the table that you want to insert.

   Word adds the table to the document.

Apply Table Styles

1. Click anywhere in the table that you want to format.

2. Click the **Design** tab on the Ribbon.

3. Click a style from the Table Styles list.

   A. *Click the **More** button (⬇) to display all the styles.*

   Word applies the style.

   B. *Toggle table parts on or off using the Table Style Options check boxes.*

   C. *Click these options to change the shading and borders.*

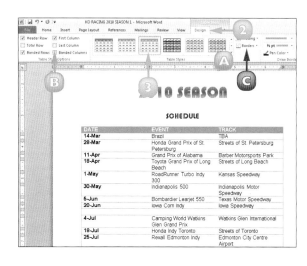

Insert an Excel Spreadsheet

1. Click in the document where you want to insert a table.

2. Click the **Insert** tab on the Ribbon.

3. Click the **Table** button.

4. Click **Excel Spreadsheet**.

   An Excel spreadsheet appears, along with tools associated with the Excel program.

5. Click in a cell and type the data that you want to add.

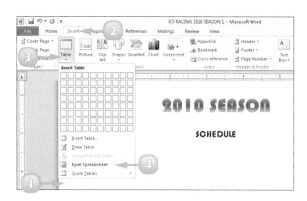

USE HEADERS, FOOTERS AND FOOTNOTES

If you want to include the same text, such as the title of your document, your name or the date, at the top or bottom of every page, you can use headers and footers. Header text appears at the very top of the page, above the margin; footer text appears at the very bottom of the page, below the margin. To view header or footer text, Word must be in Print Layout view. To switch to this view, click the **View** tab and click the **Print Layout** button.

You can include footnotes in your document. When you add a footnote, a small numeral or other character appears alongside the associated text, with the actual footnote appearing at the bottom of the page. Word automatically numbers footnotes. As you add, delete and move text, any associated footnotes are added, deleted or moved and renumbered.

Add a Header or Footer

1. Click the **Insert** tab.

2. Click the **Header** (or **Footer**) button.

3. Click the type of header or footer that you want to add.

   This example adds a header.

   A *Word adds the header or footer and displays the Header & Footer Tools tab.*

4. Click the field in the header area and type your header text.

5. If the header style includes a date, click the **Date** field and choose a date from the calendar.

   B *You can click the **Quick Parts** button to insert additional fields.*

   C *You can insert more headers and footers using these controls.*

6. Click the **Close Header and Footer** button.

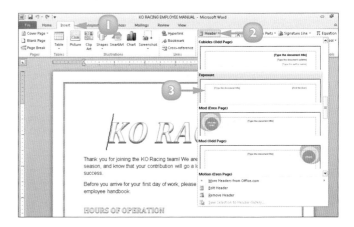

Word closes the Header & Footer Tools tab and displays the header or footer on the document page.

Insert a Footnote

 Click where you want to insert the footnote reference.

② Click the **References** tab on the Ribbon.

③ Click the **Insert Footnote** button.

REUNION

Last night I enjoyed a lovely dinner with some very old friends--people I hadn't seen in almost a decade, since before Heidi was born, let alone conceived. It was wonderful to catch up.

They live in Boston, which I am visiting on business. For one lovely semester in college, I lived here, attending Boston College and skiing for t[ ]. It was a disaster--everyone hated me. My only refuge was at the home of friends, Pepper and Stephanie, who took me in far more often than they probably would have liked. Pepper's mother had been recently divorced, and she had moved in with Pepper and Stephanie and their toddler daughter, Laura, as had two of Pepper's younger brothers, one of whom was about my age. The house was plenty full without me. But they never made me feel anything less than completely welcome. They were my family during a time when I desperately needed one.

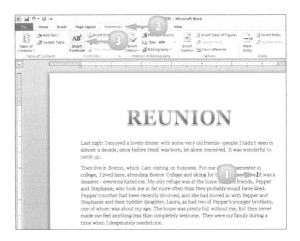

We are all older now, obviously, and it is interesting the ways in which I have "caught up" with them. When I was in college, they were in their late 20s or early 30s, doctors both, with a young daughter and a large house, and I was barely more than a child myself. They seemed terribly grown up. Now, with me in my late 30s, with a daughter of my own and my own very adult problems, we seem closer in age.

In any case, it is strange to be back in Boston. I did the math and realized it had been 18 years since I lived here, a lifetime ago, and suddenly felt very old--but also very glad that I was no longer that girl, sad and miserable. I had sort of forgotten how very lovely Boston is, what a vibrant city. It is a lovely city. I flew in yesterday morning, and as we descended we hovered briefly over the BC campus, and I clearly saw the football stadium and from there was able to pick out my old dorm.

Boston has a vibe very much its own. I spend Friday afternoon walking around (in spite of the spitting rain). I drove in and parked near Government Center, first eating a lovely Indian lunch at Faneuil Hall and then picking up the Freedom Trail, which is, essentially, a red line painted on the sidewalk. By following the line—something you do on foot—you pass by Paul Revere's house, the Old North Church (where he hung the lanterns to warn of the approaching British), a dock where the U.S.S. Constitution is moored, Bunker Hill, the Old State House (where John Adams, John Hancock, Samuel

 ¹ I had been recruited by BC to ski varsity. It wasn't until I arrived that I discovered that the primary reason I was recruited was that the person who suggested me was herself planning to leave and wanted to absolve herself of her guilt over this by finding someone (me) to replace her.

④ Type the note text.

 To return to the reference mark in the document, you can double-click the footnote number.

You can repeat these steps to add more footnotes.

 To edit a header or footer, click the Insert tab on the Ribbon, click the Header or Footer button and then click Edit Header or Edit Footer.

To omit the header or footer from the first page, click the Edit Header or Edit Footer menu option. In the Options group, select the Different First Page check box.

To remove a header or footer, click the Insert tab, click the Header or Footer button and click the Remove Header or Remove Footer command.

If you prefer, your footnotes can appear at the end of the document (endnotes). Click where you want to insert the footnote reference, click the References tab on the Ribbon and click the Insert Endnote button.

INSERT PAGE NUMBERS AND PAGE BREAKS

If you are working on a long document, you can add page numbers to help you keep the pages in order after printing the document. Page numbers are added to the header or footer area of the document. You can choose how page numbers look on your document.

Adding page breaks can help you control what text appears on what page of the document. For example, you might add a page break at the end of one chapter to ensure that the next chapter starts on a new page.

Insert Page Numbers

1. Click the **Insert** tab on the Ribbon.

2. Click the **Page Number** button.

3. Click a location for the page numbers.

4. Click a page number style.

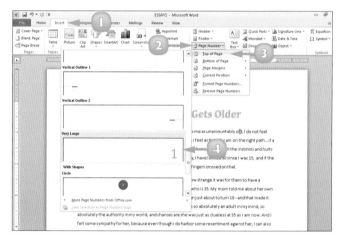

A. *Word assigns page numbers in your document.*

5. Click **Close Header and Footer** to exit the header or footer area.

Note: *See the "Use Headers, Footers and Footnotes" section to learn more.*

Insert Page Breaks

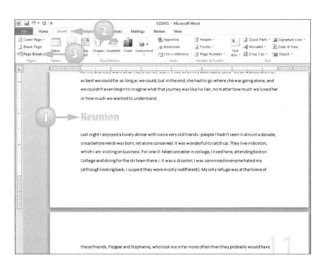

① Click in the document where you want to insert a page break.

② Click the **Insert** tab on the Ribbon.

③ Click the **Page Break** button.

Ⓑ *Word assigns the page break.*

You can use a keyboard shortcut to insert a page break as you type in your document; press Ctrl + Enter. *You can insert a line break by pressing* Shift + Enter.

You can change the page number style. Click the Page Number button on the Insert tab and then click Format Page Numbers. This opens the Page Number Format dialog box. Select the style you want.

CREATE AN INDEX

If your document requires an index, you can use Word to build one. Indexes can contain main entries and subentries as well as cross-references (entries that refer to other entries).

Before you can build an index, you must mark any words or phrases in your document that should appear in the index. When you do, Word adds a special index field, called an XE field, to the document; this field includes the marked word or phrase, as well as any cross-reference information you might have added.

Mark a Word or Phrase

① Select the text for which you want to create an index entry.

② Click the **References** tab.

③ Click the **Mark Entry** button.

Ⓐ The Mark Index Entry dialog box opens with the selected text in the Main Entry field.

Note: To create an entry for a person's name, type it in the **format** Last Name, First Name.

Ⓑ The Current Page radio button is selected.

Ⓒ To mark just this occurrence of the text, click **Mark**.

Ⓓ To mark all occurrences of the text, click **Mark All**.

Ⓔ Word adds an index entry field to your document.

Note: To view the field, click the Home tab's **Show/Hide** button (¶).

④ Click **Close**.

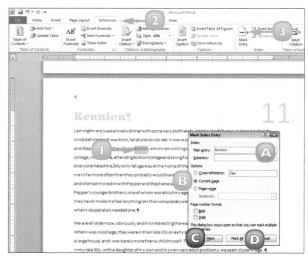

Note: To delete an index entry, select the XE field (including the braces that surround it) and press Delete.

Generate an Index

1 Click the spot in your document where you want to insert the index.

2 Click the **References** tab.

3 Click the **Insert Index** button.

The Index dialog box opens.

4 Click the **Formats** ▾ and select an index design.

A *Preview the selected index design here.*

5 Click the **Indented** radio button.

6 Click the **Columns** ⬍ to change the number of columns per page the index will contain.

7 Click **OK**.

Word generates the index.

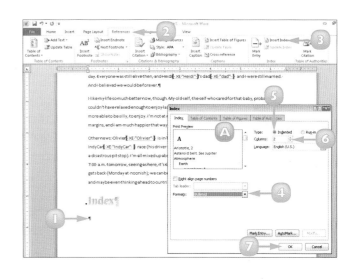

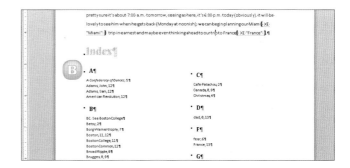

 If you want to index text that spans a range of pages, select the text and create a bookmark for it (click the Insert tab and click Bookmark). In the Mark Index Entry dialog box, click the Page range radio button. Click the Bookmark ▾ and choose the bookmark you just created, click Mark and click Close.

After making changes to your document, you need to update the index. Click in the index, click the References tab and click the Update Index button.

CREATE A TABLE OF CONTENTS

You can use Word to generate a table of contents (TOC) for your document. By default, Word generates a TOC by searching for text in your document that is formatted using one of Word's predefined heading styles. It then copies this text and pastes it into the TOC.

You can create a custom TOC based on styles you choose – handy if your document uses a template that contains heading styles that have different names from Word's predefined ones. Note that you can select from Word's gallery of TOC styles to establish the TOC's look and feel.

Style Text as Headers

1 Select text in your document that you want to style as a header.

2 Click the **Home** tab.

A *If the desired style appears in the Styles group, click it.*

B *Alternatively, click the **More** button (⏷) and choose the style from the Quick Style gallery.*

C *Alternatively, click the corner group button (▣) and choose the style from the Styles pane, as shown here.*

D *Word applies the style to the selected text.*

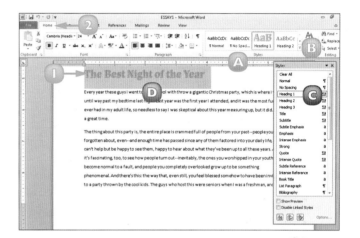

Generate a Table of Contents

1 Click the spot in your document where you want to insert a TOC.

2 Click the **References** tab.

3 Click the **Table of Contents** button.

4 Choose the desired TOC style.

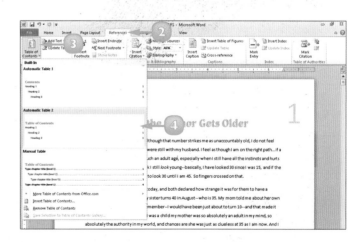

Word generates a TOC.

Note: *To delete a TOC, click the* **Table of Contents** *button and choose* **Remove Table of Contents**.

Create a TOC from Custom Styles

 Click the **References** tab.

② Click **Table of Contents.**

③ Click **Insert Table of Contents**.

④ Click **Options**.

The Table of Contents Options dialog box opens.

⑤ Under Available Styles, locate the top-level heading style you applied to your document.

⑥ Type **1** in the corresponding field to indicate that it should appear in the TOC as a level-1 heading.

Repeat Steps **5** and **6** for additional heading styles, typing **2**, **3**, **4** and so on to indicate their levels.

⑦ Click **OK** in the dialog boxes to close them.

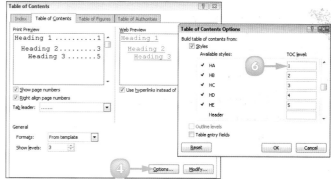

After making changes to your document, you can update the TOC to reflect the changes. Click the Update Table button in the References tab's Table of Contents group and specify whether you want to update page numbers only or the entire table.

FIND AND REPLACE TEXT

Suppose you want to edit a paragraph in your document that contains a specific word or phrase. Instead of scrolling through your document to locate that paragraph, you can use Word's Find tool to search for the word or phrase in the paragraph.

In addition, you can use the Replace tool to replace instances of a word or phrase with other text. For example, suppose you complete a long report, only to discover that you have misspelled the name of a product you are reviewing; you can use the Replace tool to locate and correct the misspellings.

Find Text

1 Click at the beginning of your document.

2 Click the **Home** tab on the Ribbon.

3 Click the **Find** button.

A *The Navigation pane appears.*

4 Type the text that you want to find and press **Enter**.

B *Word searches the document and highlights occurrences of the text.*

C *Word also lists occurrences of the text in the Navigation pane.*

5 Click an entry in the Navigation pane.

D *Word selects the corresponding text in the document.*

When finished, click the Navigation pane's **X** button.

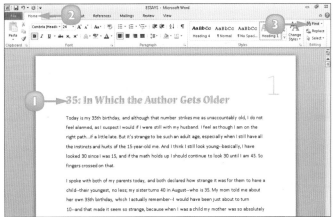

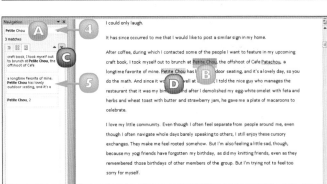

Replace Text

① Click at the beginning of your document.

② Click the **Home** tab on the Ribbon.

③ Click the **Replace** button.

The Find and Replace dialog box opens with the Replace tab shown.

④ In the **Find what** field, type the text that you want to find.

⑤ Type the replacement text in the **Replace with** field.

⑥ Click **Find Next**.

Ⓐ Word locates the first occurrence.

⑦ Click **Replace** to replace the occurrence.

Ⓑ To replace every occurrence in the document, you can click **Replace All**.

⑧ When finished, click **Cancel**.

Note: If Word displays a prompt box when the last occurrence is found, click **OK**.

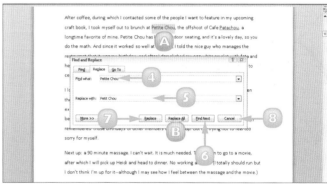

 Click More in the Find and Replace dialog box to reveal additional search options. For example, you can search for matching text case, whole words and more. You can also search for specific formatting or special characters by clicking **Format or Special**.

To search for text and delete it, type the text you want to delete in the Find What field and leave the Replace With field empty. When you activate the search, Word looks for the text and deletes it without adding new text to the document.

CHECK SPELLING AND GRAMMAR

Word automatically checks for spelling and grammar errors. Misspellings appear underlined with a red wavy line and grammar errors are underlined with a green wavy line.

In addition, you can use Word's Spelling and Grammar Check features to review your document for spelling and grammatical errors and to fix any errors that are detected. Of course, these features are no substitute for good proofreading with your own eyes. They can catch some errors, but not all!

Correct a Mistake

1 When you encounter a spelling or grammar problem, right-click the underlined text.

The menu that appears shows possible corrections.

2 Click a correction from the menu.

A *To ignore the error, click* **Ignore**; *click* **Ignore All** *for all instances of the error.*

B *To add the word to the built-in dictionary, click* **Add to Dictionary**.

Run the Spell-Checker

1 Click the **Review** tab on the Ribbon.

2 Click the **Spelling & Grammar** button.

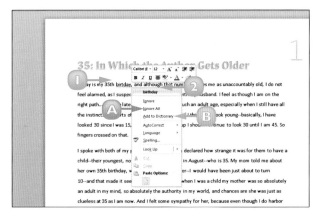

To check only a section of your document, select the section before activating the spell check.

Word searches the document for any mistakes.

 If Word finds an error, it flags it in the document and displays the Spelling and Grammar dialog box.

③ Click **Change** to make a correction.

 To correct all misspellings of this word, click **Change All**.

 To ignore the error this time, click **Ignore Once**.

 To ignore every occurrence, click **Ignore All** or **Ignore Rule**.

When the spell check is complete, a prompt box appears.

④ Click **OK**.

Turn Off Automatic Spelling and Grammar

① Click the **File** tab and then click **Options**.

② In the Word Options dialog box, click the **Proofing** tab.

③ Under the When Correcting Spelling and Grammar in Word options, click to deselect **Check spelling as you type**.

④ Click to deselect **Mark grammar errors as you type**.

⑤ Click **OK** to exit the Word Options dialog box.

Word turns off the automatic checking features.

WORK WITH AUTOCORRECT

As you may have noticed, Word automatically corrects your text as you type. It does this using its AutoCorrect feature, which works from a preset list of misspellings. To speed up your text-entry tasks, you can add your own problem words – ones you commonly misspell – to the list. The next time you mistype the word, AutoCorrect fixes your mistake for you.

If you find that AutoCorrect consistently changes a word that is correct, you can remove that word from the AutoCorrect list. If you would prefer that AutoCorrect not make any changes to your text as you type, you can disable the feature.

1. Click the **File** tab.

2. Click **Options**.

To prevent AutoCorrect from replacing text as you type, open the AutoCorrect dialog box, click the AutoCorrect tab and deselect the Replace text as you type check box. Click OK to apply your changes.

The Word Options dialog box appears.

③ Click **Proofing**.

④ Click **AutoCorrect Options**.

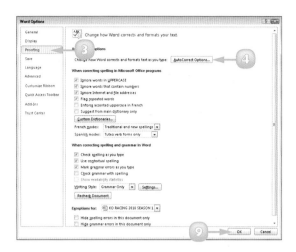

The AutoCorrect dialog box appears, displaying the AutoCorrect tab.

⑤ Type a common misspelling in the **Replace** text field.

⑥ Type the correct spelling in the **With** text field.

⑦ Click **Add**.

AutoCorrect adds the word to the list.

⑧ Click **OK** to exit the AutoCorrect dialog box.

⑨ Click **OK** to exit the Word Options dialog box.

The next time you misspell the word, AutoCorrect corrects it for you.

Note: *If AutoCorrect corrects text that you do not want to be changed, press* Ctrl *+* Z *to undo the change.*

To remove a word from the AutoCorrect list, open the AutoCorrect dialog box, click the AutoCorrect tab, click the word you want to remove and click Delete. Finally, click OK to close the dialog box and apply your changes.

If you are having trouble finding just the right word or phrase, you can use Word's thesaurus to find synonyms. Select the word for which you want to find a synonym. Click the Review tab. Click the Thesaurus button. Position your mouse pointer over the word you want to use as a replacement. Click the ▼ and click Insert.

TRACK AND REVIEW DOCUMENT CHANGES

If you share your Word documents with others, you can use the program's Track Changes feature to keep track of what edits others have made, including formatting changes and text additions or deletions.

The Track Changes feature uses different colours for each person's edits, making it easy to see who changed what in the document. If you like, you can change the colour used for your edits.

When you review the document, you can specify whose edits you want to review, what types of edits you want to see and whether to accept or reject the changes.

Turn On Tracking

① Click the **Review** tab on the Ribbon.

② Click the **Track Changes** button.

Word activates the Track Changes feature.

③ Edit the document.

Ⓐ *Additions to the text appear underlined and in colour.*

Ⓑ *Word marks deleted text with a strikethrough.*

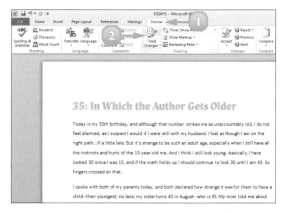

 To change the colour used for your edits, click the Review tab, click the Track Changes button and then click Change Tracking Options. The Track Changes dialog box opens and you can make changes to the tracking colour, formatting and more.

Review Changes

1 Click the **Review** tab on the Ribbon.

2 Click the **Reviewing Pane** button.

> **A** *The Reviewing pane opens.*

The Reviewing pane shows each person's edits, including the user's name.

3 Click the **Next** button.

> **B** *Word highlights the next edit in the document.*

> **C** *Click the Accept button to add the change to the final document.*

Note: *To accept all changes in the document, click the **Accept** ▾ and choose **Accept All Changes in Document**.*

> **D** *Click the **Reject** button to reject the change.*

4 When you complete the review, click the **Track Changes** button to turn the feature off.

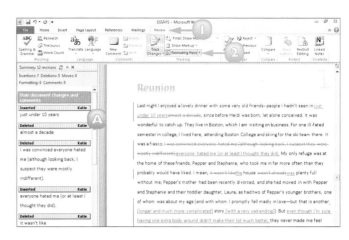

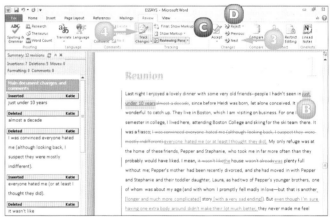

Click the Show Markup button on the Review tab to select what elements you want to include in the review. For example, you may want to hide comments or review marks for a particular user.

You can add comments to your documents, for example, to leave feedback about the text without typing directly in the document. Click or select the text where you want to insert a comment. Click the Review tab on the Ribbon and click the New Comment button. Type your comment. Word displays the comment in a balloon and in the Reviewing pane.

CONTENTS

EXCEL

Excel is a powerful spreadsheet program you can use to enter and organise data and to perform a wide variety of number-crunching tasks. You can use Excel strictly as a program for manipulating numerical data or you can use it as a database program to organise and track large quantities of data.

In this part, you learn how to enter data into worksheets, adjust its appearance, manage your information, tap into the power of Excel's formulas and functions to perform mathematical calculations and analysis, and create charts with your Excel data.

ENTER CELL DATA

You can enter data into any cell in an Excel worksheet. You can type data directly into the cell or you can enter data using the Formula bar.

Data can be text, such as row or column labels, or numbers, which are called **values**. Excel automatically left-aligns text data in a cell and right-aligns values.

Long data entries appear truncated if you type additional data into adjoining cells. You can remedy this by resizing the column to fit the data or by turning on the cell's text-wrap feature.

Type into a Cell

1 Click the cell into which you want to enter data.

The cell you clicked becomes the active cell. It appears highlighted, with a thicker border than the other cells.

A *To add data to another worksheet in your workbook, click the worksheet tab to display the worksheet.*

B *To magnify your view of the worksheet, click and drag the* **Zoom** *slider.*

2 Type your data.

C *The data appears in both the cell and the Formula bar.*

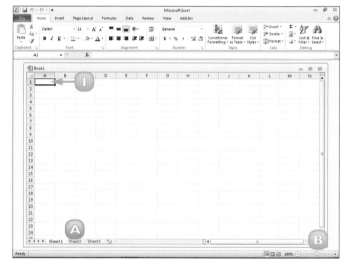

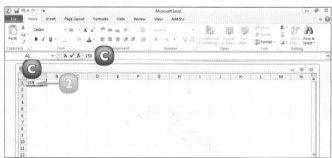

To wrap data within a cell, click the cell or cells in which you want to wrap text. Click the Wrap Text button (⊞). The height of the row increases.

Type in the Formula Bar

 Click the cell into which you want to enter data.

② Click in the Formula bar.

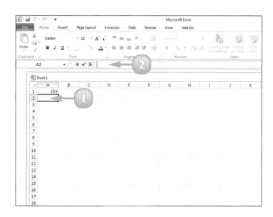

③ Type your data.

Ⓐ The data appears in both the Formula bar and the cell.

④ Click **Enter** (☑) or press Enter to enter the data.

Ⓑ To cancel an entry, you can click **Cancel** (☒) or press Esc.

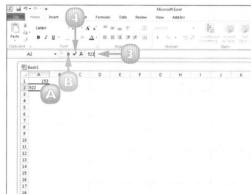

 Excel's AutoComplete feature attempts to complete entries for you, based on the first few letters that you type and other entries in the same column. If the AutoComplete entry is correct, press Enter and Excel fills in the text for you. If not, just keep typing the text that you want to insert into the cell.

You can resize columns and rows to fit the data. Position the ⌖ over the border of the heading of the column or row that you want to resize. Click and drag the border to the desired size.

SELECT CELLS

In order to perform editing, mathematical or formatting operations on data in an Excel worksheet, you must first select the cell or cells that contain that data. For example, you might apply formatting to data in a single cell or to data in a group, or **range**, of cells.

Selecting a single cell is easy: you just click the cell. To select a range of cells, you can use your mouse or keyboard. In addition to selecting cells or ranges of cells, you can select the data contained in a cell.

Select a Range of Cells

1. Click the first cell in the range of cells that you want to select.

2. Click and drag across the cells that you want to include in the range.

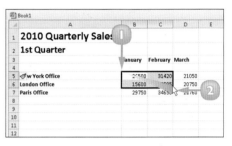

3. Release the mouse button.

   A *Excel selects the cells.*

   B *To select all of the cells in the worksheet, you can click here (▢).*

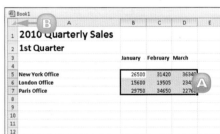

You can select multiple noncontiguous cells by pressing and holding **Ctrl** while clicking cells.

Select a Column or Row

 Position the mouse pointer over the header of the column or row that you want to select.

The ⊕ changes to ↓.

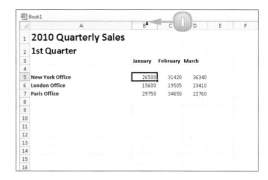

 Click the column or row.

Excel selects the entire column or row.

To select multiple columns or rows, you can click and drag across the column or row headings.

You can select multiple noncontiguous columns or rows by pressing and holding **Ctrl** while clicking column or row headings.

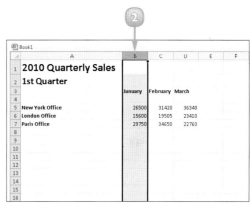

To select data inside a cell, click the cell; then click in front of the data in the Formula bar and drag over the characters or numbers you want to select. Alternatively, click the cell and then double-click the data you want to select.

*You can also use the keyboard to select a range. Navigate to the first cell in the range. Press and hold **Shift** while using an arrow key, such as ← or ↓, to select the remaining cells in the range.*

FASTER DATA ENTRY WITH AUTOFILL

You can use Excel's AutoFill feature to add duplicate entries or a data series to your worksheet. This can greatly expedite data entry.

You can use Excel's built-in lists of common entries to create text series – for example, to enter a list containing the days of the week or months in the year – or number series. You can also create your own custom data lists,

When you click a cell, a small fill handle appears in the lower right corner of the selector; you use this to create an AutoFill series.

AutoFill a Text Series

① Type the first entry in the text series.

② Click and drag the cell's fill handle across or down the number of cells that you want to fill.

The ⬧ changes to +.

You can also use AutoFill to copy the same text to every cell that you drag over.

③ Release the mouse button.

Ⓐ AutoFill fills in the text series.

Ⓑ An AutoFill smart tag (⊞) may appear, offering additional options that you can assign to the data.

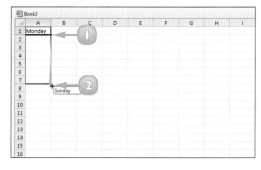

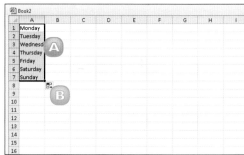

AutoFill a Number Series

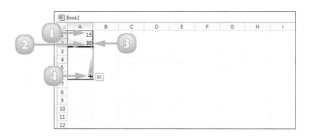

1. Type the first entry in the number series.

2. In an adjacent cell, type the next entry in the series.

3. Select both cells.

Note: See the "Select Cells" section to learn more.

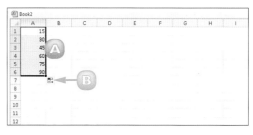

4. Click and drag the fill handle across or down the number of cells that you want to fill.

   The ⊕ changes to +.

5. Release the mouse button.

   Ⓐ AutoFill fills in the number series.

   Ⓑ An AutoFill smart tag (⊞) may appear, offering additional options that you can assign to the data.

Create a Custom List

1. Create the custom list (here, a list of names) in your worksheet and select the cells containing the list.

2. Click the **File** tab and then click the **Options** button.

3. In the Options dialog box, click the **Advanced** tab.

4. Click the **Edit Custom Lists** button.

5. Click **Import**.

6. Click **OK**.

87

CHANGE THE FONT AND SIZE

You can change the font that you use for your worksheet data, along with the size of the data. For example, you may want to make the worksheet title larger than the rest of the data or you may want to resize the font for the entire worksheet to make the data easier to read. Alternatively, you might choose to apply a specific colour to certain types of data.

If you particularly like the result of applying a series of formatting options to a cell, you can copy the formatting and apply it to other cells your worksheet.

① Select the data that you want to format.

Change the Font

② Click the **Home** tab on the Ribbon.

③ Click the **Font** ▾.

Ⓐ You can use the scroll arrows or scroll bar to scroll through the available fonts.

You can also begin typing a font name to choose a font.

④ Click a font.

Excel applies the font.

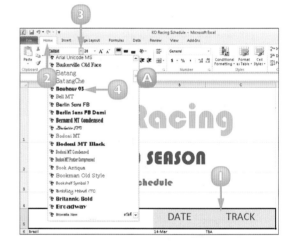

Change the Font Size

② Click the **Home** tab on the Ribbon.

③ Click the **Font Size** ▾.

④ Click a size.

Excel applies the new size to the selected cell or data.

CHANGE NUMBER FORMATS

You can use number formatting to control the appearance of numerical data in your worksheet. For example, if you have a column of prices, you can format the data as numbers with pound signs and decimal points. If prices listed are in a currency other than pounds, you can indicate that as well.

Excel offers several different number categories, or styles, to choose from. These include Currency styles, Accounting styles, Date styles, Time styles, Percentage styles and more. You can apply number formatting to single cells, ranges, columns, rows or an entire worksheet.

1. Select the cell, range or data that you want to format.

2. Click the **Home** tab on the Ribbon.

3. Click the **Number Format** ▼.

4. Click a number format.

   Excel applies the number format to the data.

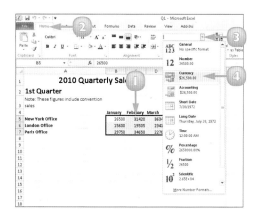

A. *Click the **Accounting Number Format** button (⑤) to apply pound signs to your data. Click the button's down arrow to specify a different currency, such as Euro.*

B. *To add percent signs to your data, click the **Percent Style** button (%).*

C. *To apply commas to your number data, click the **Comma Style** button (⑨).*

D. *Click the corner group button (⬛) to open the Format Cells dialog box, with more number-formatting options.*

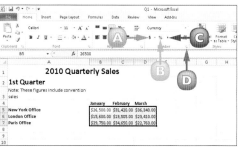

 To control the number of decimal places that appear in numeric data, select the cell or range that you want to format. Click the Home tab on the Ribbon. Click Increase Decimal (⬛) or Decrease Decimal (⬛).

APPLY CONDITIONAL FORMATTING

You can use Excel's Conditional Formatting tool to apply certain formatting attributes, such as bold text or a fill colour, to a cell when the value of that cell meets the required condition. For example, if your worksheet tracks weekly sales, you might set up Excel's Conditional Formatting tool to alert you if a sales figure falls below what is required for you to break even. In addition to using preset conditions, you can create your own. To help you distinguish the degree to which various cells meet your conditional rules, you can use colour scales and data bars.

Apply a Conditional Rule

① Select the cell or range to which you want to apply conditional formatting.

② Click the **Home** tab on the Ribbon.

③ Click the **Conditional Formatting** button.

④ Click **Highlight Cells Rules**.

⑤ Click the type of rule that you want to create.

A rule dialog box appears.

⑥ Specify the values that you want to assign for the condition.

⑦ Click **OK**.

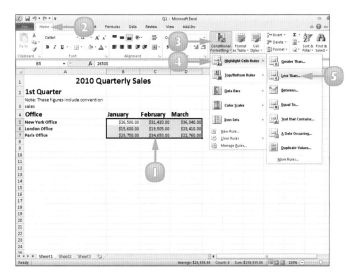

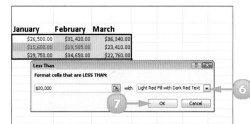

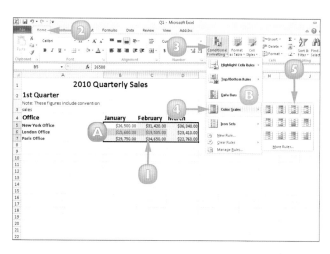

A *If the value of a selected cell meets the condition, Excel applies the conditional formatting.*

Apply a Colour Scale

 Select the cell or range that contains the conditional formatting.

② Click the **Home** tab on the Ribbon.

③ Click the **Conditional Formatting** button.

④ Click **Color Scales**.

⑤ Click a colour scale.

    B *You can apply colour bars instead by clicking **Data Bars**.*

    C *Excel applies the colour scale to the conditional formatting.*

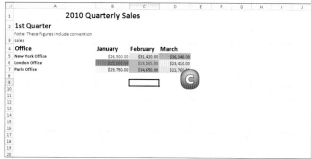

To create a new rule for conditional formatting, click the **Conditional Formatting** button on the Home tab and then click **New Rule** to open the **New Formatting Rule** dialog box. Here, you define the condition of the rule as well as what formatting you want to apply when the condition is met.

To remove conditional formatting from a cell, select the data that contains the formatting you want to remove, click the **Conditional Formatting** button on the Home tab and then click **Manage Rules**. Next, click the rule you want to remove, click **Delete Rule** and click OK.

ADD COLUMNS AND ROWS

You can add columns and rows to your worksheets to include more data. For example, you might need to add a column or row in the middle of several existing columns or rows to add data that you left out the first time you created the workbook.

With Excel, you can add columns and rows using the Insert button on the Ribbon or using the Insert dialog box.

You are not limited to inserting new columns and rows one at a time; if you want, you can insert multiple new columns and rows at once.

Add a Column

1. Click the heading of the column to the right of where you want to insert a new column.

2. Click the **Home** tab on the Ribbon.

3. Click the **Insert** ▾.

4. Click **Insert Sheet Columns**.

Note: You can also right-click a column heading and click **Insert**.

A. *Excel adds a column.*

B. *A smart tag icon ( ) may appear when you insert a column; click it to view a list of options that you can apply.*

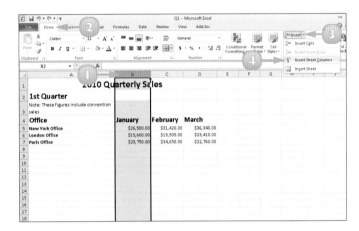

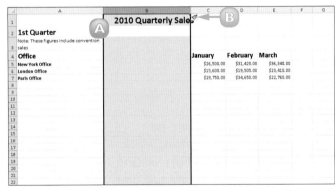

Add a Row

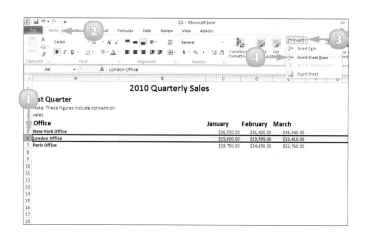

1. Click the heading of the row below where you want to insert a new row.

2. Click the **Home** tab on the Ribbon.

3. Click the **Insert** ▾.

4. Click **Insert Sheet Rows**.

Note: You can also right-click a row heading and click **Insert**.

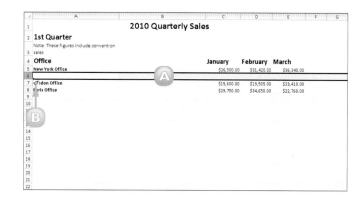

A. Excel adds a row.

B. A smart tag icon () may appear and you can click the icon to view a list of options that you can assign.

✓ To insert multiple columns and rows, select two or more columns and rows in the worksheet; then activate the Insert command as described in this section. Excel adds the same number of new columns and rows as the number you originally selected.

✓ To open the Insert dialog box, click a cell, click the Insert ▾ on the Home tab and click Insert Cells. Then click Entire Row or Entire Column and click OK. Excel adds a row or column above or to the left of the active cell.

FREEZE A COLUMN OR ROW

You can freeze portions of your worksheet to keep them visible as you scroll to view other data. This is especially handy in large worksheets. For example, you might freeze a column or row to keep the labels in view as you scroll to other areas of your worksheet to view the data in that column or row. You cannot scroll the area that you freeze, but you can scroll the unfrozen areas of the worksheet. When you are finished viewing these other areas of your worksheet, you can unfreeze the column or row you froze.

① Click the cell to the right of the column or below the row that you want to freeze.

② Click the **View** tab on the Ribbon.

③ Click the **Freeze Panes** ▾.

④ Click **Freeze Panes**.

You can also choose to freeze a row of column headings or a column of row titles.

Excel freezes the areas above or to the left of the selected cell (depending on whether you are scrolling up and down or left and right).

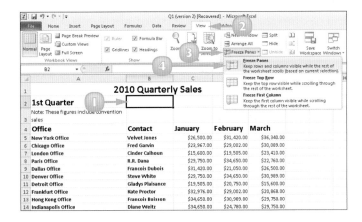

To unlock the columns and rows, click the Freeze Panes ▾ and then click Unfreeze Panes.

NAME A RANGE

You can assign distinctive names to the cells and ranges of cells that you work with in a worksheet. (A *range* is simply a rectangular group of related cells; a range can consist of a single cell.) Assigning names to cells and ranges makes it easier to identify their contents and can also help you when deciphering formulas. (Formulas are discussed in Chapter 10.)

① Select the cells comprising the range that you want to name.

② Click the **Formulas** tab on the Ribbon.

③ Click the **Define Name** button.

The New Name dialog box opens.

④ Type a name for the selected range in the **Name** field.

Ⓐ You can add a comment or note about the range here. For example, you might indicate what data the range contains.

⑤ Click **OK**.

Ⓑ Excel assigns the name to the cells.

To go to a range, click the Name ▾ and click the name of the range of cells to which you want to move.

DELETE DATA OR CELLS

You can delete Excel data that you no longer need. When you decide to delete data, you can choose whether you want to remove the data from the cells but keep the cells in place or delete the cells entirely. When you delete a cell's contents, Excel removes only the data. When you delete a cell entirely, Excel removes the cell as well as its contents, with the existing cells in your worksheet shifting over to fill any gap in the worksheet structure. In addition to deleting single cells, you can delete whole rows or columns.

Delete Data

1. Select the cell or cells containing the data that you want to remove.

2. Press **Delete**.

   Excel deletes the data from the cell, but the cell remains.

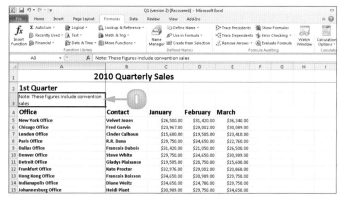

Delete Cells

1. Select the cell or cells that you want to remove.

2. Click the **Home** tab.

3. Click the **Delete** [▼].

4. Click **Delete Cells**.

Note: You can also right-click the selected cells and then click the **Delete** command.

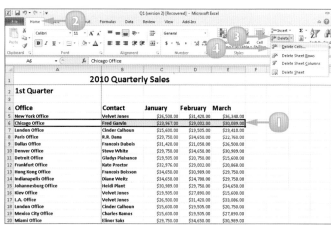

The Delete dialog box appears.

⑤ Click a deletion option.

⑥ Click **OK**.

	A		B	C	D	E
1			**2010 Quarterly Sales**			
2	**1st Quarter**					
3						
4	**Office**		**Contact**	**January**	**February**	**March**
5	New York Office		Velvet Jones	$26,500.00	$31,420.00	$36,340.00
6	Chicago Office		Fred Garvin	$23,967.00	$29,002.00	$30,089.00
7	London Office		Cinder Calhoun	$15,600.00	$19,505.00	$23,410.00
8	Paris Office		R.R. Dana	$29,750.00	$34,650.00	$22,760.00
9	Dallas Office		Francois Dubo	21,050.00	$26,500.00
10	Denver Office		Steve White	34,650.00	$30,989.00
11	Detroit Office		Gladys Plaisan	20,750.00	$15,600.00
12	Frankfurt Office		Kate Proctor	002.00	$20,868.00
13	Hong Kong Office		Francois Boiss	0,989.00	$29,750.00
14	Indianapolis Office		Diane Weitz	24,780.00	$29,750.00
15	Johannesburg Office		H lant	29,750.00	$34,650.00
16	Kiev Office		ones	27,890.00	$15,600.00
17	L.A. Office		Velvet Jones	$26,500.00	$31,420.00	$33,086.00
18	London Office		Cinder Calhoun	$15,600.00	$19,505.00	$20,750.00
19	Mexico City Office		Charles Ramos	$15,600.00	$19,505.00	$27,890.00
20	Miami Office		Elinor Saks	$29,750.00	$34,650.00	$30,989.00
21	Milan Office		Jess Bova	$15,600.00	$19,505.00	$27,890.00
22	Minneapolis Office		James Stanton	$29,002.00	$20,868.00	$32,976.00

Delete dialog box: Delete — Shift cells left / ● Shift cells up ⑤ / Entire row / Entire column — OK Cancel ⑥

Excel removes the cells and their content from the worksheet.

Other cells shift over or up to fill the void of any cells that you remove from your worksheet.

	A		B	C	D	E
1			**2010 Quarterly Sales**			
2	**1st Quarter**					
3						
4	**Office**		**Contact**	**January**	**February**	**March**
5	New York Office		Velvet Jones	$26,500.00	$31,420.00	$36,340.00
6	London Office		Cinder Calhoun	$15,600.00	$19,505.00	$23,410.00
7	Paris Office		R.R. Dana	$29,750.00	$34,650.00	$22,760.00
8	Dallas Office		Francois Dubois	$31,420.00	$21,050.00	$26,500.00
9	Denver Office		Steve White	$29,750.00	$34,650.00	$30,989.00
10	Detroit Office		Gladys Plaisance	$19,505.00	$20,750.00	$15,600.00
11	Frankfurt Office		Kate Proctor	$32,976.00	$29,002.00	$20,868.00
12	Hong Kong Office		Francois Boisson	$34,650.00	$30,989.00	$29,750.00
13	Indianapolis Office		Diane Weitz	$34,650.00	$24,780.00	$29,750.00
14	Johannesburg Office		Heidi Plant	$30,989.00	$29,750.00	$34,650.00
15	Kiev Office		Velvet Jones	$19,505.00	$27,890.00	$15,600.00
16	L.A. Office		Velvet Jones	$26,500.00	$31,420.00	$33,086.00
17	London Office		Cinder Calhoun	$15,600.00	$19,505.00	$20,750.00
18	Mexico City Office		Charles Ramos	$15,600.00	$19,505.00	$27,890.00
19	Miami Office		Elinor Saks	$29,750.00	$34,650.00	$30,989.00
20	Milan Office		Jess Bova	$15,600.00	$19,505.00	$27,890.00
21	Minneapolis Office		James Stanton	$29,002.00	$20,868.00	$32,976.00
22	Montreal Office		Jacqueline Pfeiffer	$33,086.00	$22,588.00	$29,389.00

*To delete a whole column or row, click the column or row heading to select it; then click the **Delete** button in the Home tab. Excel deletes any existing data within the selected column or row and moves subsequent columns or rows to fill the space left by the deletion.*

*To remove a cell's formatting without removing the content, select the cell you want to edit, click the **Home** tab, click the **Clear** button (✐) and choose **Clear Formats** to remove the cell's formatting.*

ADD A WORKSHEET

By default, when you create a new workbook in Excel, it contains three worksheets. This may be adequate in some cases, but if your workbook requires additional worksheets in which to enter more data, you can easily add them. For example, if your workbook contains data about products your company sells, you might add worksheets for each product category.

1 Click the **Insert Worksheet** button (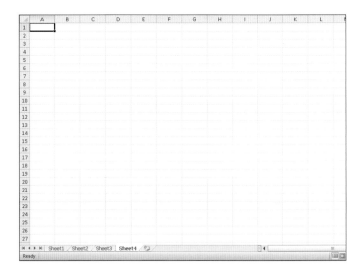).

You can also right-click a worksheet tab and click **Insert** to open the Insert dialog box, where you can choose to insert a worksheet.

	A	B	C	D	E	F
1		2010 Quarterly Sales				
2	1st Quarter					
3						
4	Office	Contact	January	February	March	
5	New York Office	Velvet Jones	$26,500.00	$31,420.00	$36,340.00	
6	London Office	Cinder Calhoun	$15,600.00	$19,505.00	$23,410.00	
7	Paris Office	R.R. Dana	$29,750.00	$34,650.00	$22,760.00	
8	Dallas Office	Francois Dubois	$31,420.00	$21,050.00	$26,500.00	
9	Denver Office	Steve White	$29,750.00	$34,650.00	$30,989.00	
10	Detroit Office	Gladys Plaisance	$19,505.00	$20,750.00	$15,600.00	
11	Frankfurt Office	Kate Proctor	$32,976.00	$29,002.00	$20,868.00	
12	Hong Kong Office	Francois Boisson	$34,650.00	$30,989.00	$29,750.00	
13	Indianapolis Office	Diane Weitz	$34,650.00	$24,780.00	$29,750.00	
14	Johannesburg Office	Heidi Plant	$30,989.00	$29,750.00	$34,650.00	
15	Kiev Office	Velvet Jones	$19,505.00	$27,890.00	$15,600.00	
16	L.A. Office	Velvet Jones	$26,500.00	$31,420.00	$33,086.00	
17	London Office	Cinder Calhoun	$15,600.00	$19,505.00	$20,750.00	
18	Mexico City Office	Charles Ramos	$15,600.00	$19,505.00	$27,890.00	
19	Miami Office	Elinor Saks	$29,750.00	$34,650.00	$30,989.00	
20	Milan Office	Jess Bova	$15,600.00	$19,505.00	$27,890.00	
21	Minneapolis Office	James Stanton	$29,002.00	$20,868.00	$32,976.00	
22	Montreal Office	Jacqueline Pfeiffer	$33,086.00	$22,588.00	$29,389.00	
23	Mumbai Office	Katie Kitchel	$27,890.00	$15,600.00	$19,505.00	
24	New York Office	Velvet Jones	$26,500.00	$31,420.00	$21,050.00	
25	Paris Office	R. R. Dana	$29,750.00	$34,650.00	$24,780.00	
26	Phoenix Office	Velvet	$32,976.00	$29,002.00	$20,868.00	

Sheet1 Sheet2 Sheet3
Ready

2 Excel adds a new worksheet and gives it a default worksheet name.

Sheet1 Sheet2 Sheet3 Sheet4
Ready

NAME A WORKSHEET

When you create a new workbook, Excel assigns a default name to each worksheet in the workbook. Likewise, Excel assigns a default name to each worksheet you add to an existing workbook.

To help you identify their content, you can change the names of your Excel worksheets to something more descriptive. For example, if your workbook contains four worksheets, each detailing a different sales quarter, then you can give each worksheet a unique name, such as Quarter 1, Quarter 2 and so on.

① Double-click the worksheet tab that you want to rename.

Excel highlights the current name.

You can also right-click the worksheet name and click **Rename**.

	A	B	C	D	E	F
1		2010 Quarterly Sales				
2	1st Quarter					
3						
4	Office	Contact	January	February	March	
5	New York Office	Velvet Jones	$26,500.00	$31,420.00	$36,340.00	
6	London Office	Cinder Calhoun	$15,600.00	$19,505.00	$23,410.00	
7	Paris Office	R.R. Dana	$29,750.00	$34,650.00	$22,760.00	
8	Dallas Office	Francois Dubois	$31,420.00	$21,050.00	$26,500.00	
9	Denver Office	Steve White	$29,750.00	$34,650.00	$30,989.00	
10	Detroit Office	Gladys Plaisance	$19,505.00	$20,750.00	$15,600.00	
11	Frankfurt Office	Kate Proctor	$32,976.00	$29,002.00	$20,868.00	
12	Hong Kong Office	Francois Boisson	$34,650.00	$30,989.00	$29,750.00	
13	Indianapolis Office	Diane Weitz	$34,650.00	$24,780.00	$29,750.00	
14	Johannesburg Office	Heidi Plant	$30,989.00	$29,750.00	$34,650.00	
15	Kiev Office	Velvet Jones	$19,505.00	$27,890.00	$15,600.00	
16	L.A. Office	Velvet Jones	$26,500.00	$31,420.00	$33,086.00	
17	London Office	Cinder Calhoun	$15,600.00	$19,505.00	$20,750.00	
18	Mexico City Office	Charles Ramos	$15,600.00	$19,505.00	$27,890.00	
19	Miami Office	Elinor Saks	$29,750.00	$34,650.00	$30,989.00	
20	Milan Office	Jess Bova	$15,600.00	$19,505.00	$27,890.00	
21	Minneapolis Office	James Stanton	$29,002.00	$20,868.00	$32,976.00	
22	Montreal Office	Jacqueline Pfeiffer	$33,086.00	$22,588.00	$29,389.00	
23	Mumbai Office	Katie Kitchel	$27,890.00	$15,600.00	$19,505.00	
24	New York Office	Velvet Jones	$26,500.00	$31,420.00	$21,050.00	
25	Paris Office	R. R. Dana	$29,750.00	$34,650.00	$24,780.00	
26	Phoenix Office	Velvet Jones	$32,976.00	$29,002.00	$20,868.00	

Sheet1 Sheet2 Sheet3 Sheet4

Ready

② Type a new name for the worksheet.

③ Press **Enter**.

Excel assigns the new worksheet name.

	A	B	C	D	E	F
1		2010 Quarterly Sales				
2	1st Quarter					
3						
4	Office	Contact	January	February	March	
5	New York Office	Velvet Jones	$26,500.00	$31,420.00	$36,340.00	
6	London Office	Cinder Calhoun	$15,600.00	$19,505.00	$23,410.00	
7	Paris Office	R.R. Dana	$29,750.00	$34,650.00	$22,760.00	
8	Dallas Office	Francois Dubois	$31,420.00	$21,050.00	$26,500.00	
9	Denver Office	Steve White	$29,750.00	$34,650.00	$30,989.00	
10	Detroit Office	Gladys Plaisance	$19,505.00	$20,750.00	$15,600.00	
11	Frankfurt Office	Kate Proctor	$32,976.00	$29,002.00	$20,868.00	
12	Hong Kong Office	Francois Boisson	$34,650.00	$30,989.00	$29,750.00	
13	Indianapolis Office	Diane Weitz	$34,650.00	$24,780.00	$29,750.00	
14	Johannesburg Office	Heidi Plant	$30,989.00	$29,750.00	$34,650.00	
15	Kiev Office	Velvet Jones	$19,505.00	$27,890.00	$15,600.00	
16	L.A. Office	Velvet Jones	$26,500.00	$31,420.00	$33,086.00	
17	London Office	Cinder Calhoun	$15,600.00	$19,505.00	$20,750.00	
18	Mexico City Office	Charles Ramos	$15,600.00	$19,505.00	$27,890.00	
19	Miami Office	Elinor Saks	$29,750.00	$34,650.00	$30,989.00	
20	Milan Office	Jess Bova	$15,600.00	$19,505.00	$27,890.00	
21	Minneapolis Office	James Stanton	$29,002.00	$20,868.00	$32,976.00	
22	Montreal Office	Jacqueline Pfeiffer	$33,086.00	$22,588.00	$29,389.00	
23	Mumbai Office	Katie Kitchel	$27,890.00	$15,600.00	$19,505.00	
24	New York Office	Velvet Jones	$26,500.00	$31,420.00	$21,050.00	
25	Paris Office	R. R. Dana	$29,750.00	$34,650.00	$24,780.00	
26	Phoenix Office	Velvet Jones	$32,976.00	$29,002.00	$20,868.00	

1st Quarter Sheet2 Sheet3 Sheet4

Ready

CHANGE PAGE SETUP OPTIONS

You can assign various settings related to page setup settings to your Excel worksheets. These include settings for changing the worksheet's orientation, margins, paper size and more. For example, if your workbook data is too wide to fit on a standard sheet of paper, you might change the page orientation from Portrait, which is the default in Excel, to Landscape in order to fit more data on the page horizontally. You can also use Excel's page setup settings to insert your own page breaks to control the placement of data on a printed page.

Change the Page Orientation

1 Click the **Page Layout** tab on the Ribbon.

2 Click the **Orientation** button.

3 Click **Portrait** or **Landscape**.

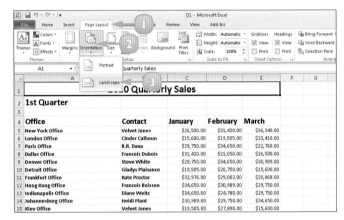

Excel applies the new orientation. This example applies Landscape.

A Excel marks the edge of the page with a dotted line.

B You can click the **Margins** button to set up page margins.

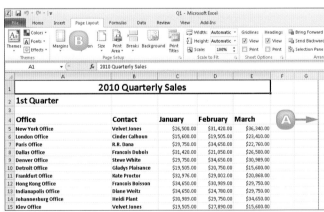

Insert a Page Break

 1 Select the row above which you want to insert a page break.

2 Click the **Page Layout** tab on the Ribbon.

3 Click the **Breaks** button.

4 Click **Insert Page Break**.

Excel inserts a page break.

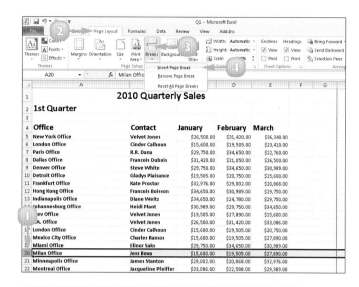

 A *Excel marks the edge of the page with a dotted line.*

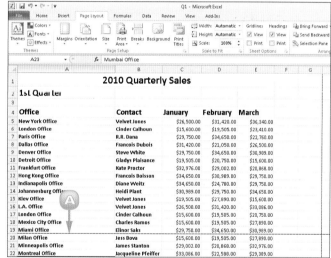

✓ *To print only a portion of a worksheet, select the cells that you want to print, click the Page Layout tab on the Ribbon, click the Print Area button and click Set Print Area. Then print as normal.*

✓ *By default, the gridlines that you see on a worksheet do not print with the cell data. To turn on gridlines for printing, select the Print check box under Gridlines on the Page Layout tab. A check mark in the check box indicates that the feature is on.*

MOVE AND COPY WORKSHEETS

You can move a worksheet within a workbook to rearrange the worksheet order. For example, you may want to position the worksheet that you use most often as the first worksheet in the workbook or you might move a worksheet you rarely view to be the last worksheet in the workbook.

In addition to moving worksheets within a workbook, you can copy them. You might copy a worksheet to use it as a starting point for data that is new, yet similar. When you copy a worksheet, Excel assigns it a default name: the original worksheet's name followed by a number, starting with (2).

1 Click the tab of the worksheet that you want to move or copy.

2 Move or copy the worksheet to the desired spot.

To move the worksheet, drag it to a new position in the list of worksheets. (The ▷ changes to ▷.)

To copy the worksheet, press and hold **Ctrl** and drag the worksheet copy to a new position in the list of worksheets. (The ▷ changes to ▷.)

A *A small black triangle icon keeps track of the worksheet's location in the group while you drag.*

3 Release the mouse button.

B *Excel moves or copies the worksheet. (Here, the worksheet was moved.)*

9	Denver Office	Steve White	$29,750.00
10	Detroit Office	Gladys Plaisance	$19,505.00
11	Frankfurt Office	Kate Proctor	$32,976.00
12	Hong Kong Office	Francois Boisson	$34,650.00
13	Indianapolis Office	Diane Weitz	$34,650.00
14	Johannesburg Office	Heidi Plant	$30,989.00
15	Kiev Office	Velvet Jones	$19,505.00
16	L.A. Office	Velvet Jones	$26,500.00
17	London Office	Cinder Calhoun	$15,600.00
18	Mexico City Office	Charles Ramos	$15,600.00
19	Miami Office	Elinor Saks	$29,750.00
20	Milan Office	Jess Bova	$15,600.00
21	Minneapolis Office	James Stanton	$29,002.00
22	Montreal Office	Jacqueline Pfeiffer	$33,086.00
23	Mumbai O...	Katie Kitchel	$27,890.00
24	Phoenix O...	Velvet Jones	$32,976.00
25	Rio Office	Murgatroyd Peterso	$34,298.00
26	San Francisco Office	Betsy Shoun	$18,939.00

I◄ ◄ ► ►I   1st Quarter / 2nd Quarter / 3rd Quarter / 4th Quarter
Ready

8	Dallas Office	Francois Dubois	$31,420.00
9	Denver Office	Steve White	$29,750.00
10	Detroit Office	Gladys Plaisance	$19,505.00
11	Frankfurt Office	Kate Proctor	$32,976.00
12	Hong Kong Office	Francois Boisson	$34,650.00
13	Indianapolis Office	Diane Weitz	$34,650.00
14	Johannesburg Office	Heidi Plant	$30,989.00
15	Kiev Office	Velvet Jones	$19,505.00
16	L.A. Office	Velvet Jones	$26,500.00
17	London Office	Cinder Calhoun	$15,600.00
18	Mexico City Office	Charles Ramos	$15,600.00
19	Miami Office	Elinor Saks	$29,750.00
20	Milan Office	Jess Bova	$15,600.00
21	Minneapolis Office	James Stanton	$29,002.00
22	Montreal Office	Jacqueline Pfeiffer	$33,086.00
23	Mumbai Office	Katie Kitchel	$27,890.00
24	Phoenix Office	Velvet Jones	$32,976.00
25	Rio Office	Murgatroyd Peterso	$34,298.00
26	San Francisco Office	Betsy Shoun	$18,939.00

I◄ ◄ ► ►I   2nd Quarter   1st Quarter / 3rd Quarter / 4th Quarter
Ready

DELETE A WORKSHEET

You can delete a worksheet that you no longer need in your workbook. For example, you might delete a worksheet that contains outdated data or information about a product that your company no longer sells.

When you delete a worksheet, Excel prompts you to confirm the deletion unless the worksheet is blank, in which case it simply deletes the worksheet.

You should always check the worksheet's contents before deleting it to avoid removing any important data. As soon as you delete a worksheet, Excel permanently removes it from the workbook file.

① Right-click the worksheet tab.

② Click **Delete**.

Note: *You can also click the **Delete** ▾ on the Home tab and then click **Delete**.*

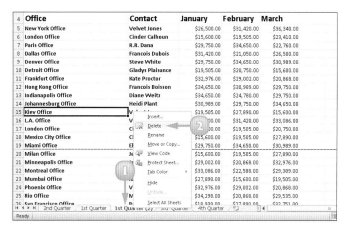

If the worksheet contains any data, Excel prompts you to confirm the deletion.

③ Click **Delete**.

Excel deletes the worksheet.

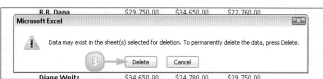

FIND AND REPLACE DATA

Suppose you want to locate a particular number, formula, word or phrase in your Excel worksheet. Rather than using the scroll bars in the Excel program window to scroll through your worksheet and locate that information, you can use the Find tool.

In addition to using the Find tool to find data, you can use the Replace tool to replace instances of text or numbers with other data. For example, suppose you discover that you have consistently misspelled the name of a product in your worksheet, you can use the Replace tool to locate and correct the misspellings.

Find Data

① Click the **Home** tab on the Ribbon.

② Click the **Find & Select** button.

③ Click **Find**.

The Find and Replace dialog box appears, displaying the Find tab.

④ Type the data you want to find.

⑤ Click **Find Next**.

Ⓐ *Excel finds the first occurrence of the data.*

You can click **Find Next** again to search for the next occurrence.

⑥ When finished, click **Close** to close the dialog box.

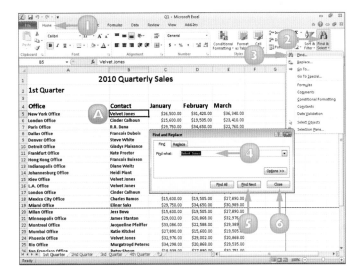

Replace Data

① Click the **Home** tab on the Ribbon.

② Click the **Find & Select** button.

③ Click **Replace**.

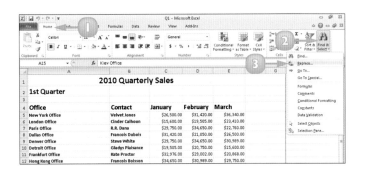

The Find and Replace dialog box appears, displaying the Replace tab.

 Type the data that you want to find.

 Type the replacement data.

 Click **Find Next**.

 Excel locates the first occurrence of the data.

 Click **Replace** to replace it.

 *You can click **Replace All** to replace every occurrence in the worksheet.*

 Excel replaces the data with the text you typed.

 Excel selects the next instance of the data.

 When finished, click **Close**.

Note: *Excel may display a prompt box when the last occurrence is found. Click **OK**.*

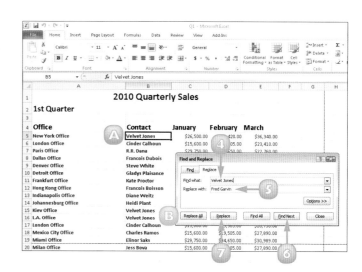

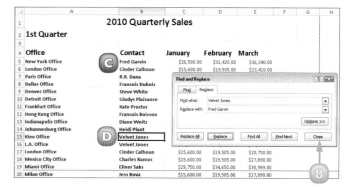

 Click the Options button in the Find and Replace dialog box to reveal additional search options. For example, you can search by rows or columns, matching data and more. You can also search for specific formatting or special characters using Format options.

 To search for data and delete it, start by typing the text in the Find what field. Leave the Replace with field empty. When you activate the search, Excel looks for the data and deletes it without adding new data to the worksheet.

SORT DATA

You can sort your Excel data to reorganise the information. This technique is particularly useful when using Excel to create database tables. A *database table* is a list of related information. Tables contain *fields* – typically columns – to break the list into manageable pieces. Each entry in the list is called a *record*. Rows contain each record in your list of data.

For example, you might want to sort a client table to list the names alphabetically. Ascending order sorts list records from A to Z or from lowest number to highest number; descending order sorts list records from Z to A or from highest number to lowest number.

Perform a Quick Sort

① Click in the field name or heading, that you want to sort.

② Click the **Home** tab on the Ribbon.

③ Click the **Sort & Filter** button.

④ Click an ascending or descending sort command.

> **Ⓐ** *Excel sorts the records.*

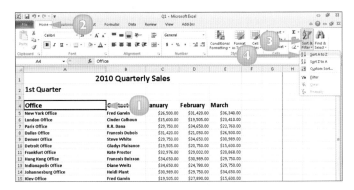

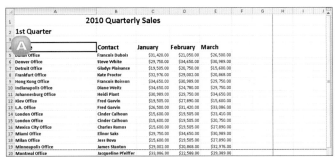

Perform a Custom Sort

1. Click in the worksheet you want to sort.

2. Click the **Home** tab on the Ribbon.

3. Click the **Sort & Filter** button.

4. Click **Custom Sort**.

   The Sort dialog box appears.

5. Click the first **Sort by** [▼] and select the primary field to sort by.

   A *By default, the Sort On field is set to Values. To sort on another setting, you can click the **Sort On** [▼] and choose a setting.*

6. Click the **Order** [▼] to sort the field in ascending or descending order.

   B *To specify additional sort fields, click **Add Level** and repeat Steps **5** and **6**.*

7. Click **OK**.

   C *Excel sorts the data.*

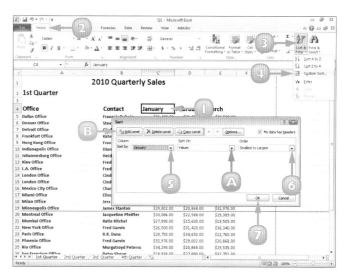

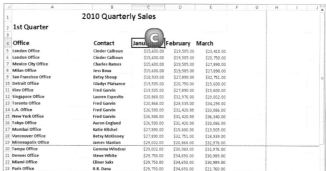

107

Most database tables place related data in columns but some place this data in rows. If you want to sort data across a row, click in the worksheet, click the Home tab, click the Sort & Filter button and choose Custom Sort to open the Sort dialog box. Then click the Options button. In the Sort Options dialog box that appears, click Sort Left to Right.

FILTER DATA

If you are using Excel as a database, you can use an AutoFilter to view only portions of your data. When you sort data, the entire table is sorted. (Refer to the previous section, "Sort Data," to learn how to sort data in Excel.) In contrast, when you apply an AutoFilter, only certain records are shown based on criteria you set. Any records that do not match the criteria are hidden. For example, you might set up an AutoFilter to display only those data records containing a particular value in the postcode field.

① Select the field names for the data you want to filter.

② Click the **Home** tab on the Ribbon.

③ Click the **Sort & Filter** button.

④ Click **Filter**.

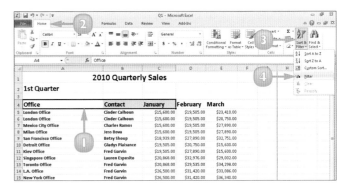

Ⓐ Excel adds drop-down arrow buttons (▾) to your field names.

⑤ Click a field's ▾.

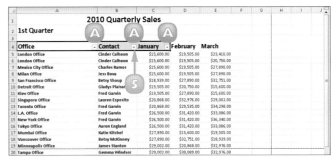

6 Click the data you want to use as a filter.

7 Click **OK**.

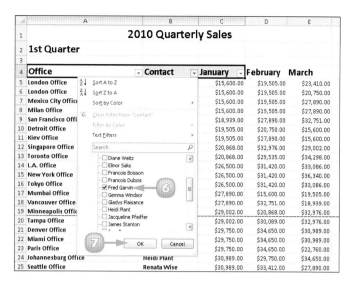

B *Excel filters the table.*

To view all the records again, click the **Sort & Filter** button in the Home tab and choose **Clear**.

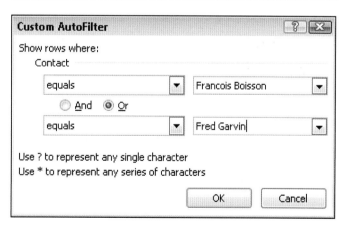

Customise a Filter

1 Click ▾ next to the field by which you want to filter.

2 Click **Text Filters** or **Number Filters.**

3 Click **Custom Filter**.

In the Custom AutoFilter dialog box, you can select operators and values to apply to the filtered data. In this case, the filter displays all records whose Contact field contains the values Francois Boisson or Fred Garvin.

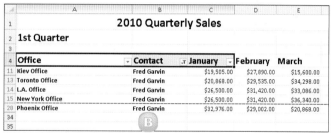

CREATE A FORMULA

You can write a formula to perform a calculation on data in your worksheet. In Excel, all formulas begin with an equals sign (=) and contain the cell references of the cells that contain the relevant data. (Note that in addition to referring to cells in the current worksheet, you can also build formulas that refer to cells in other worksheets.) For example, the formula for adding the contents of cells C3 and C4 together is **=C3+C4**. You create formulas in the Formula bar; formula results appear in the cell to which you assign a formula.

① Click in the cell to which you want to assign a formula.

② Type **=**.

    Ⓐ *Excel displays the formula in the Formula bar and in the active cell.*

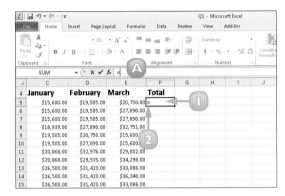

③ Click the first cell that you want to reference in the formula.

    Ⓑ *Excel inserts the cell reference into the formula.*

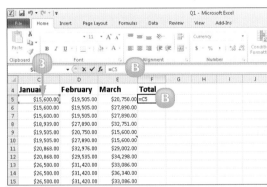

4 Type an operator such as + or −.

5 Click the next cell that you want to reference in the formula.

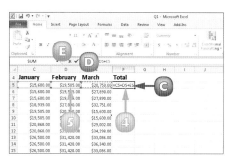

C *Excel inserts the cell reference into the formula.*

6 Repeat Steps **4** and **5** until all the necessary cells and operators have been added.

7 Press Enter.

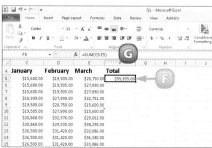

D *You can also click **Enter** (☑) on the Formula bar to accept the formula.*

E *You can click **Cancel** (☒) to cancel the formula.*

F *The formula results appear in the cell.*

To view the formula in the Formula bar, you can simply click in the cell.

G *The Formula bar displays any formula assigned to the active cell.*

Note: *If you change a value in a cell referenced in your formula, the formula results automatically update to reflect the change.*

 To edit a formula, click in the cell containing the formula and make any corrections in the Formula bar. Alternatively, double-click in the cell to make edits to the formula from within the cell itself. When finished, press Enter or click Enter (☑) on the Formula bar.

 To reference a cell in another worksheet, specify the worksheet name followed by an exclamation mark and then the cell address (for example, Sheet2!D12 or Sales!D12). If the worksheet name includes spaces, enclose the sheet name in single quote marks, as in 'Sales Totals'!D12.

APPLY ABSOLUTE AND RELATIVE CELL REFERENCES

By default, Excel uses *relative cell referencing*. That is, it treats the location of cells that you include in formulas as relative rather than absolute. If you copy a formula to a new location, the cell references in that formula adjust accordingly.

If you want to refer to a particular cell regardless of where the formula appears, you can assign an absolute cell reference. For example, suppose you have a formula that refers to a discount rate disclosed in cell G10. Even if you move that formula, it must always reference cell G10 – meaning the cell reference G10 should be absolute.

Assign an Absolute Reference

1. Click in the cell containing the formula that you want to change.

2. Select the cell reference in the Formula bar.

3. Press F4.

Note: You can also type dollar signs in the Formula bar to make a reference absolute.

A. Excel enters dollar signs ($) before each part of the cell reference, making the cell reference absolute.

Note: You can continue pressing F4 to cycle through mixed, relative and absolute references.

4. Press Enter or click **Enter** (☑).

Excel assigns the changes to the formula.

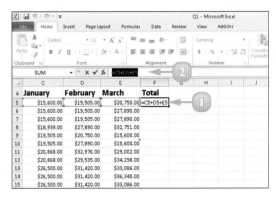

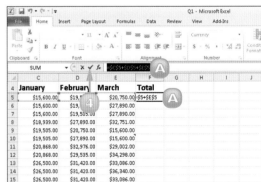

Assign a Relative Reference

 Click in the cell containing the formula that you want to change.

2 Select the cell reference.

3 Press **F4** as many times as needed to cycle to relative addressing (that is, remove the dollar signs).

Note: You can press **F4** multiple times to cycle through mixed, relative and absolute references.

Note: You can also delete the dollar sign characters in the Formula bar to make a reference relative.

4 Press **Enter** or click **Enter** (✓).

A Excel assigns the changes to the formula.

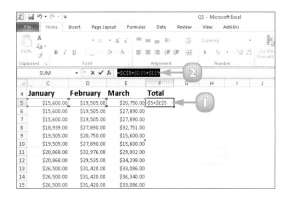

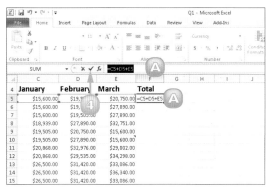

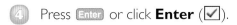

✓ **You use mixed referencing to reference the same row or column, but different relative cells in it. For example, referencing $C6 keeps the column absolute whereas the row remains relative. If the mixed reference is C$6, the column is relative but the row is absolute.**

UNDERSTANDING FUNCTIONS

If you are looking for a speedier way to enter formulas, you can use any one of a wide variety of functions. *Functions* are ready-made formulas that perform a series of operations on a specified range of values. Excel offers more than 300 functions, grouped into 12 categories, that you can use to perform mathematical calculations on your worksheet data.

Functions use arguments to indicate what cells contain the values you want to calculate. Functions can refer to individual cells or to ranges of cells. This section explains the basics of working with functions.

Function Elements

All functions start with an equals sign (=). Functions are distinct in that each one has a name. For example, the function that sums data is called SUM. You can use functions by typing them directly into your worksheet cells or Formula bar; you can also use the Insert Function dialog box to select and apply functions to your data.

Types of Function

Excel groups functions into 12 categories, each of which includes a variety of functions:

Category	Description
Financial	Includes functions for calculating loans, principal, interest, yield and depreciation.
Date & Time	Includes functions for calculating dates, times and minutes.
Math & Trig	Includes a wide variety of functions for calculations of all types.
Statistical	Includes functions for calculating averages, probabilities, rankings, trends and more.
Lookup & Reference	Includes functions that enable you to locate references or specific values in your worksheets.
Database	Includes functions for counting, adding and filtering database items.
Text	Includes text-based functions to search and replace data and other text tasks.
Logical	Includes functions for logical conjectures, such as if-then statements.
Information	Includes functions for testing your data.
Engineering	Offers many functions for engineering calculations.
Cube	Enables Excel to fetch data from SQL Server Analysis Services, such as members, sets, aggregated values, properties and KPIs.
Compatibility	Use these functions to keep your workbook compatible with earlier versions of Excel.

Common Functions

The following table lists some of the more popular Excel functions that you might use with your own spreadsheet work.

Function	Category	Description	Syntax
SUM	Math & Trig	Adds values	=SUM(number1,number2,...)
INT	Math & Trig	Rounds down to the nearest integer	=INT(number)
ROUND	Math & Trig	Rounds a number to a specified number of digits	=ROUND(number,number_digits)
ROUNDDOWN	Math & Trig	Rounds a number down	=ROUNDDOWN(number,number_digits)
COUNT	Statistical	Counts the number of cells in a range that contain data	=COUNT(value1,value2,...)
AVERAGE	Statistical	Averages a series of arguments	=AVERAGE(number1,number2,...)
MIN	Statistical	Returns the smallest value in a series	=MIN(number1,number2,...)
MAX	Statistical	Returns the largest value in a series	=MAX(number1,number2,...)
MEDIAN	Statistical	Returns the middle value in a series	=MEDIAN(number1,number2,...)
PMT	Financial	Finds the periodic payment for a fixed loan	=PMT(interest_rate,number_of_periods,present_value,future_value,type)
RATE	Financial	Returns an interest rate	=RATE(number_of_periods,payment,present_value,future_value,type,guess)
TODAY	Date & Time	Returns the current date	=TODAY()
IF	Logical	Returns one of two results that you specify based on whether the value is true or false	=IF(logical_text,value_if_true,value_if_false)
AND	Logical	Returns true if all of the arguments are true, false if any is false	=AND(logical1,logical2,...)
OR	Logical	Returns true if any argument is true, false if all arguments are false	=OR(logical1,logical2,...)

Constructing Arguments

Arguments are enclosed in parentheses. When applying a function to individual cells in a worksheet, you can use a comma to separate the cell addresses, as in **=SUM(A5,B5,C5)**. When applying a function to a range of cells, you can use a colon to designate the first and last cells in the range, as in **=SUM(B5:E12)**. If your range has a name, you can insert the name, as in **=SUM(Sales)**.

APPLY A FUNCTION

You use the Insert Function dialog box to look for a particular function from among Excel's 300-plus available functions. Functions are divided into 12 categories: Financial, Date & Time, Math & Trig, Statistical, Lookup & Reference, Database, Text, Logical, Information, Engineering, Cube and Compatibility.

After you have selected your function, you build the formula using the Function Arguments dialog box. Functions use arguments to indicate the cells that contain the values you want to calculate.

① Click in the cell to which you want to assign a function.

② Click the **Formulas** tab on the Ribbon.

③ Click the **Insert Function** button.

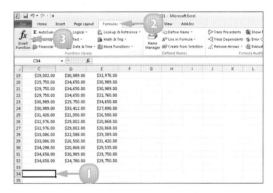

Ⓐ *Excel inserts an equals sign to denote a formula.*

Excel launches the Insert Function dialog box.

④ Click the **Or select a category** ▼ and choose a function category.

Ⓑ *A list of functions in the selected category appears.*

⑤ Click the function that you want to apply.

Ⓒ *A description of the selected function appears here.*

⑥ Click **OK**.

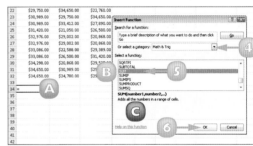

The Function Arguments dialog box appears.

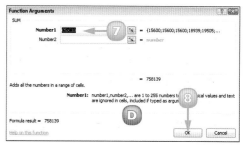

7 Select the cells for each argument required by the function.

If you select a cell or range of cells directly in the worksheet, Excel automatically adds the references to the argument.

You can also type a range or cell address (or range or cell name) into the various text boxes.

D The dialog box displays additional information about the function here.

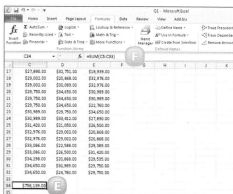

8 When you finish constructing the arguments, click **OK**.

E Excel displays the function results in the cell.

F The function appears in the Formula bar.

 To edit a function, click the cell containing the function that you want to edit, click the Formulas *tab and click the* Insert Function *button. Excel displays the function's Function Arguments dialog box, where you can change the cell references or values as needed.*

 Click the Help on this function *link in the Insert* Function or Function Arguments *dialog box to access Excel's help files. The function's help includes an example of the function being used and tips about how to use the function.*

TOTAL CELLS WITH AUTOSUM

One of the most popular Excel functions is the AutoSum function. AutoSum automatically totals the contents of cells. For example, you can quickly total a column of sales figures.

One way to use AutoSum is to select a cell and let the function guess which surrounding cells you want to total. Alternatively, you can specify exactly which cells to sum.

① Click in the cell where you want to insert a sum total.

② Click the **Formulas** tab on the Ribbon.

③ Click the **AutoSum** button.

Ⓐ *If you click the **AutoSum** ▾, you can select another common function, such as Average.*

You can also click the **AutoSum** button (**Σ**) on the Home tab.

Ⓑ *AutoSum generates a formula to total the adjacent cells.*

④ Press **Enter** or click **Enter** (✓).

Excel displays the AutoSum result in the cell.

✓ **You can get a quick total of cells without applying a function. Click the cells whose values you want to total. In the status bar along the bottom of the program window, Excel displays the sum, the number of cells and the average of the selected cells.**

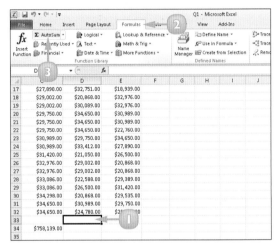

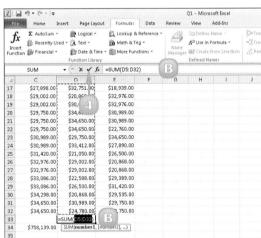

AUDIT A WORKSHEET FOR ERRORS

On occasion, you may see an error message, such as #DIV/0!, in your Excel worksheet. If you do, you should double-check your formula references to ensure that you have referenced the correct cells. Locating the source of an error is difficult, however – especially in larger worksheets. Fortunately, if an error occurs in your worksheet, you can use Excel's Formula Auditing tools – Error Checking and Trace Error – to examine and correct formula errors.

1. Click the **Formulas** tab on the Ribbon.

2. Click the **Error Checking** button.

   A *Excel displays the Error Checking dialog box and highlights the first cell containing an error.*

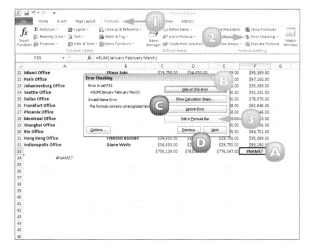

3. To fix the error, click **Edit in Formula Bar**.

   B *To find help with an error, you can click here to open the help files.*

   C *To ignore the error, you can click* **Ignore Error**.

   D *You can click* **Previous** *and* **Next** *to scroll through all of the errors on the worksheet.*

4. Make edits to the cell references in the Formula bar.

5. Click **Resume**.

   When the error check is complete, a prompt box appears.

6. Click **OK**.

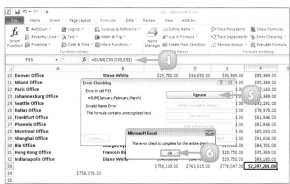

CREATE A CHART

You can quickly convert your spreadsheet data into easy-to-read charts. You can choose from a wide variety of chart types to suit your needs, including column, line, pie, bar, area, scatter, stock, surface, doughnut, bubble and radar charts. Excel makes it easy to determine exactly what type of chart works best for your data.

After you create a chart, you can use the Chart Tools on the Ribbon to fine-tune the chart to best display and explain the data.

① Select the range of data that you want to chart.

You can include any headings and labels, but do not include subtotals or totals.

② Click the **Insert** tab on the Ribbon.

③ Click a chart type from the Charts group.

④ Click a chart style.

Ⓐ *Excel creates a chart and places it in the worksheet.*

Ⓑ *You can click the **Design** tab to find tools for controlling design elements in the chart, such as the chart layout, style and type.*

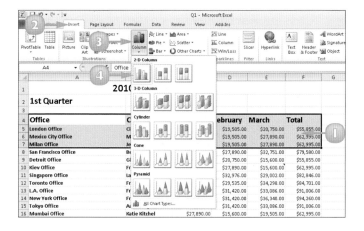

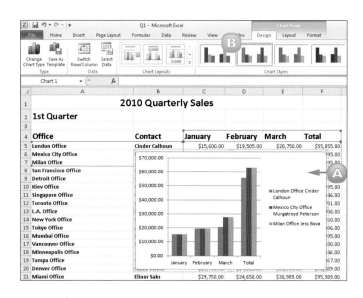

120

You can click the **Layout** tab to find tools for controlling how the chart elements are positioned on the chart.

 You can click the **Format** tab to find tools for formatting various chart elements, including chart text and shapes.

 You can add an organisational chart to track the hierarchy of an organisation or a process. Click the Insert tab and then click the SmartArt button. When you insert an organisational chart, Excel creates four shapes to which you can add your own text; you can add additional shapes and branches to the chart as needed.

 To include noncontiguous cells and ranges In a chart, select the first cell or range and then press and hold `Ctrl` while selecting additional cells and ranges.

CONTENTS

POWERPOINT

PowerPoint is a presentation program you can use to convey all kinds of messages to an audience. You can use PowerPoint to create slide shows to present ideas to clients, explain a concept or procedure to employees or teach a class. In this part, you learn how to create slide shows; add text, tables, charts, video clips and pictures to your slide show; and package your show on a CD-ROM or output it as a movie file. You also learn how to add special effects, including animations, sound effects, and transitions to make your slide show lively and engaging.

CREATE A PHOTO ALBUM PRESENTATION

You can quickly turn any collection of digital photos on your computer into a slide show presentation in PowerPoint. For example, you might compile your photos from a recent vacation into a presentation. Alternatively, you might gather your favourite photos of a friend or loved one in a presentation. To liven up the presentation, you can include captions with your photos. You can also vary the layout of slides, including having one (the default), two, three or more photos per slide. You can then share the presentation with others or e-mail the file to family and friends.

① Click the **Insert** tab on the Ribbon.

② Click **Photo Album**.

③ Click **New Photo Album**.

The Photo Album dialog box appears.

④ Click the **File/Disk** button.

The Insert New Pictures dialog box appears.

⑤ Navigate to the folder or drive containing the digital pictures that you want to use.

⑥ Click the pictures that you want to use.

To use multiple pictures, you can press and hold **Ctrl** while clicking the pictures that you want to use.

⑦ Click **Insert**.

A *You can change the order of pictures using these buttons.*

B *To remove a picture, you can click it in the Pictures in the album list and then click* **Remove**.

C *You can use the tool buttons to change the picture orientation, contrast and brightness levels.*

8 Click **Create**.

D *PowerPoint creates the slide show as a new presentation file.*

Note: *The first slide in the show is a title slide, containing the title "Photo Album" and your user name.*

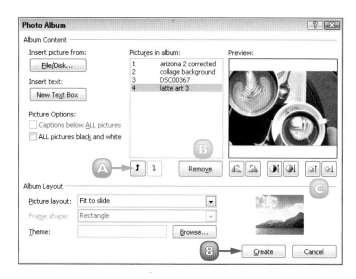

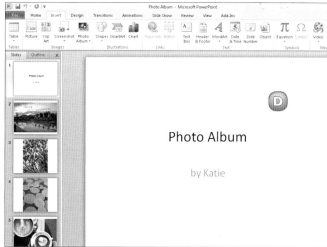

 Select the Captions Below All Pictures check box in the Photo Album dialog box to add captions. Alternatively, add a text slide after each photo slide by clicking the New Text Box button. Type your captions after closing the Photo Album dialog box.

 By default, PowerPoint displays one picture per slide, but you can use the Picture Layout setting in the Photo Album dialog box to display as many as four, with or without title text.

CREATE A PRESENTATION WITH A TEMPLATE

You can use PowerPoint's templates to help you create a new presentation, regardless of its subject matter. PowerPoint installs with a wide variety of presentation templates featuring various designs and colour schemes.

In addition to using templates that come preinstalled with Office, if your computer is connected to the Internet, you can download PowerPoint templates from Office.com for use with your presentations.

① Click the **File** tab.

② Click **New**.

③ Click **Sample templates**.

   Ⓐ *You can click **New from existing** to create a new presentation based on the template of an existing one.*

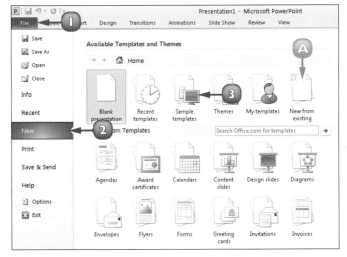

④ Click a template.

   Ⓑ *PowerPoint displays a preview of the template design.*

⑤ Click **Create**.

PowerPoint creates the presentation using the template you chose and displays it in Normal view. You can add your own text to each slide. .

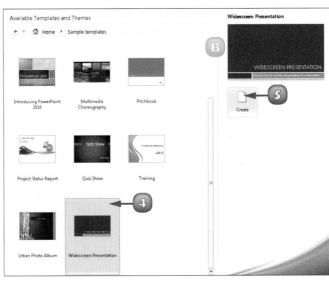

BUILD A BLANK PRESENTATION

Whenever you start PowerPoint, it displays a blank slide. You can use this blank slide as the first slide in your presentation, adding more slides and formatting them as needed. Alternatively, if you are already working on a presentation, you can create a new blank presentation from scratch using the File menu.

Building a presentation in this manner rather than choosing from one of PowerPoint's existing templates allows you the freedom to create your own colour schemes and apply your own design touches. If you build a presentation that you particularly like, you can save it as a template for future use.

1 Click the **File** tab.

2 Click **New**.

3 Click **Blank presentation**.

4 Click **Create**.

PowerPoint creates a new presentation with one blank slide.

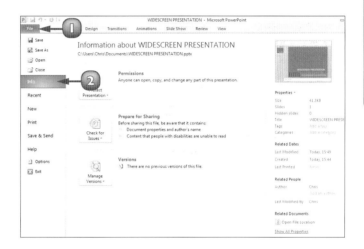

 If you create a presentation that you particularly like you can turn that presentation into a template file that you can reuse. Click the File tab and then click Save As. In the Save As dialog box, click the Save as type ▾ and choose PowerPoint Template. Type a name for the template in the File name field and click Save. PowerPoint saves the presentation as a template.

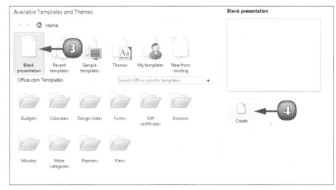

CHANGE POWERPOINT VIEWS

You can use PowerPoint's views to change how your presentation appears on-screen. By default, PowerPoint displays your presentation in Normal view, with the Slides tab showing the order of slides in your presentation. You can view the Outline tab to see your presentation in an outline format or switch to Slide Sorter view to see all the slides at the same time.

In addition to changing PowerPoint views, you can use the PowerPoint zoom settings to change the magnification of a slide. You can also change the size of the panes in the PowerPoint window, making them larger or smaller as needed.

Use Outline View

1 While in Normal view, click the **Outline** tab.

PowerPoint displays the presentation in an outline format.

A *You can click the outline text to edit it.*

B *You can click a slide icon to view the slide.*

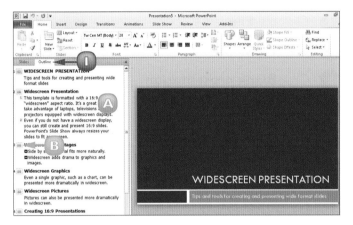

Use Slides View

1 Click the **Slides** tab.

A *PowerPoint displays the current slide in the presentation.*

B *To view a particular slide, you can click the slide in the Slides tab.*

C *To close the tabs pane entirely and free up on-screen workspace, you can click the* ✗.

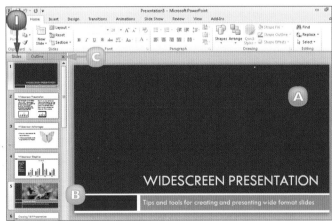

Note: *To redisplay the tabs pane, click the* **View** *tab on the Ribbon and then click the* **Normal** *button.*

Use Slide Sorter View

1. Click the **View** tab.

2. Click the **Slide Sorter** button.

   PowerPoint displays all of the slides in the presentation.

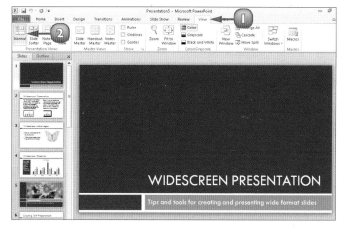

Use Normal View

1. Click the **View** tab.

2. Click the **Normal** button.

   PowerPoint returns to the default view, displaying the current slide in the presentation.

 To change the magnification of a slide, you can drag the Zoom bar on the status bar at the bottom of the PowerPoint window. Alternatively, click the View tab, click the Zoom button and choose the desired magnification in the Zoom dialog box. Click the Fit to Window button to return to the default view.

 To resize the PowerPoint panes, position the mouse pointer over the pane's border. The ⬚ changes to ⬚. Click and drag inward or outward to resize the pane.

INSERT SLIDES

PowerPoint makes it easy to add more slides to a presentation. To add a slide, you use the New Slide button on the Home tab.

Clicking the top half of the New Slide button adds a slide with the same layout as the one selected in the Slides pane; alternatively, you can click the bottom half of the button and select a different layout. You can add and remove slides on the Slides tab in Normal view or you can switch to Slide Sorter view to manage your presentation's slides.

① In the Slides pane, click the slide after which you want to insert a new slide.

② Click the **Home** tab.

③ Click the bottom half of the **New Slide** button.

④ Click a slide design.

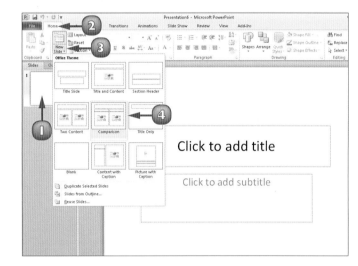

Ⓐ *PowerPoint adds a new slide.*

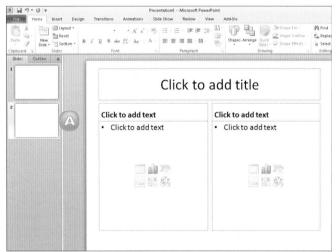

CHANGE THE SLIDE LAYOUT

PowerPoint includes several predefined slide layouts that you can apply to your slide. For example, you might apply a layout that includes a title with two content sections or a picture with a caption.

For best results, you should assign a new layout before adding content to your slides; otherwise, you may need to make a few adjustments to the content's position and size to fit the new layout. In addition to using PowerPoint's predefined slide layouts, you can also create your own custom layouts.

1 Click the slide whose layout you want to change in the Slides tab.

2 Click the **Home** tab on the Ribbon.

3 Click the **Layout** button.

4 Click a layout.

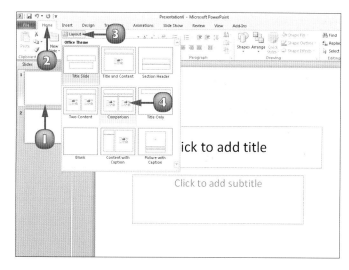

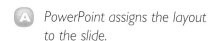

 A PowerPoint assigns the layout to the slide.

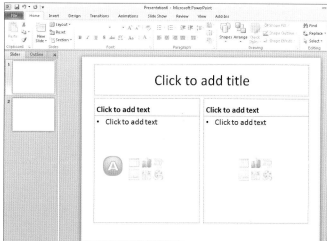

To create a custom layout, click the View tab on the Ribbon and click the Slide Master button. In the Slide Master pane, click the Insert Layout button on the Slide Master tab. Click the bottom half of the Insert Placeholder button, click a slide object type and click and drag to set the object's size and placement.

ADD AND EDIT SLIDE TEXT

When you apply one of PowerPoint's text layouts to a slide, the text box appears with placeholder text. You can replace the placeholder text with your own text. You can do so either typing directly in the slide, as described in this section or typing in the Outline tab that appears in the pane on the left side of the screen. After you add your text, you can change its font, size, colour and more, as shown in the next section.

Add Slide Text

① Click the text box to which you want to add text.

PowerPoint hides the placeholder text and displays a cursor.

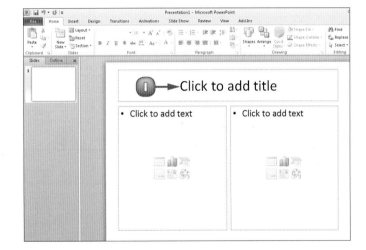

② Type the text that you want to add.

Edit Slide Text

① Click in the text box where you want to edit.

PowerPoint selects the text box and adds a cursor to the text box.

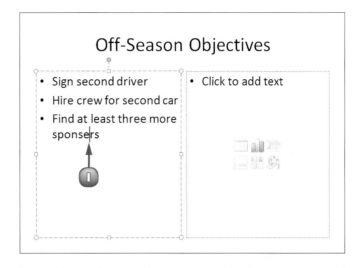

② Make any changes that you want to the slide text.

You can use the keyboard arrow keys to move the cursor in the text or you can click where you want to make a change.

Add Text using the Outline Tab

① Click the **Outline** tab.

② Click the slide that you want to edit.

③ Type the text that you want to add or change.

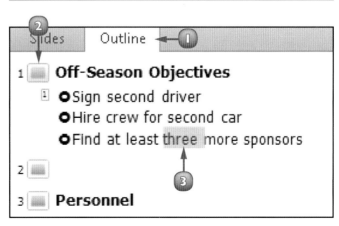

CHANGE THE FONT, SIZE AND COLOUR

After you add text to a slide (as described in the preceding section, "Add and Edit Slide Text"), you can change the slide text's font, size, colour and style to alter its appearance. For example, you might choose to increase the size of a slide's title text in order to draw attention to it or change the font of the body text to match the font used in your company logo. Alternatively, you might change the text's colour to make it stand out against the background colour. You can also apply formatting to the text, such as bold, italics, underlining, shadow or strikethrough.

Change the Font

① Select the text that you want to edit.

② Click the **Home** tab on the Ribbon.

③ Click the **Font** ▾.

④ Click a font.

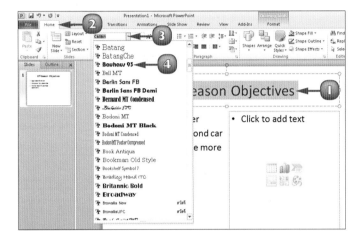

PowerPoint applies the font you chose to the selected text.

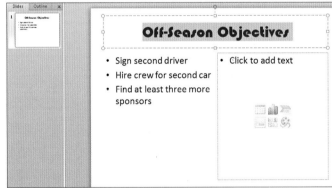

134

Change the Size

① Select the text that you want to edit.

② Click the **Home** tab on the Ribbon.

③ Click the **Font Size** ▾.

④ Click a size.

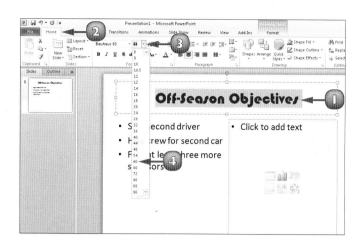

PowerPoint applies the font size you chose to the selected text.

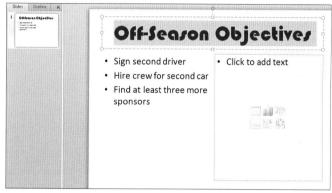

 To quickly increase or decrease the font size, you can select the text you want to change and then click the Increase Font Size (A⌃) or Decrease Font Size (A⌄) button in the Home tab's Font group as many times as needed until the text is the desired size.

 Select the text whose format you want to change and then click the Bold button (B), the Italic button (I), the Underline button (U), the Shadow button (S) or the Strikethrough button (abc).

continued ➡

135

CHANGE THE FONT, SIZE AND COLOUR *(continued)*

In addition to changing the text's font and size, you can change its colour. You might do so to make the text better stand out against the background or to coordinate with colours used in other slide elements such as photographs.

You can change the text colour using a number of methods. One is to select a colour from the Font Color button on the Home tab; another is to launch the Colors dialog box and select a colour from the palette that appears. In addition, you can apply your own custom colour to text.

Choose a Coordinating Colour

1 Select the text that you want to edit.

2 Click the **Home** tab on the Ribbon.

3 Click the ▾ next to the **Font Color** button ( ).

A *PowerPoint displays coordinating theme colours that go with the current slide design.*

4 Click a colour.

PowerPoint applies the colour you chose to the selected text.

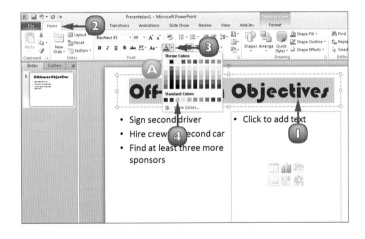

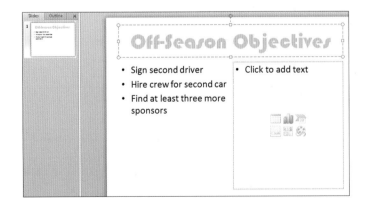

Open the Colors Dialog Box

1 Select the text that you want to edit.

2 Click the **Home** tab on the Ribbon.

3 Click the ▼ next to the **Font Color** button (⊞).

4 Click **More Colors**.

The Colors dialog box appears.

5 Click the **Standard** tab.

6 Click a colour.

7 Click **OK**.

PowerPoint applies the colour you chose to the selected text.

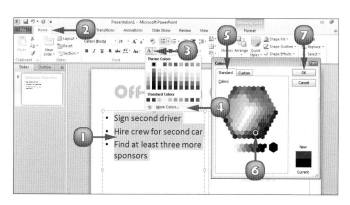

Set a Custom Colour

1 Open the Colors dialog box and click the **Custom** tab.

2 Click the colour that you want to customise.

3 Drag the intensity arrow to adjust the colour intensity.

A *You can also adjust the colour channel settings.*

4 Click **OK**.

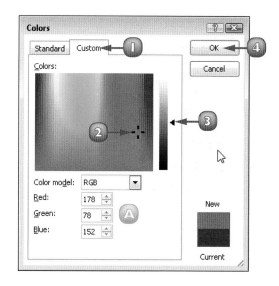

You can apply a theme to give every slide in your presentation the same look and feel. Click the Design tab. Click the More button (▼) to view the full palette of themes. Right-click a theme from the Themes group. Choose Apply to All Slides or Apply to Selected Slides.

SET LINE SPACING

You can change the line spacing in a PowerPoint slide to create more or less space between lines of text in the slide. For example, you might want to increase line spacing from the default 1.0 setting to a setting such as 2.0 or even 3.0 so the text fills up more space in the text box or to make the text easier to read. If, after increasing line spacing, you find that your text does not quite fit in its text box, you can reduce the line spacing to make room. You access PowerPoint line-spacing options from the Home tab.

① Select the text that you want to edit.

② Click the **Home** tab on the Ribbon.

③ Click the 🔽 next to the **Line Spacing** button (📑).

④ Click a line spacing amount.

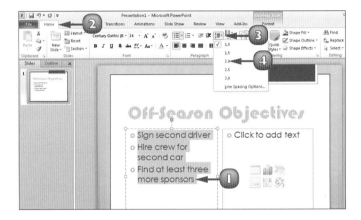

PowerPoint applies the line spacing.

Ⓐ *This example shows 2.0 spacing.*

You can change the alignment of text. Select the text that you want to edit and click the Home tab on the Ribbon. Click an alignment button: Align Left (▤), Center (▤), Align Right (▤) or Justify (▤).

ADD A TEXT BOX TO A SLIDE

You may choose to insert slides containing a predefined layout. You can customise the slide layout, however, by adding a new text box to it. A text box is simply a receptacle for text in a slide. (For help adding text to a text box, refer to the section "Add and Edit Slide Text" earlier in this chapter.)

When you add a new text box to a slide, you can control the placement and size of the box. (For help moving and resizing text boxes and other slide objects, see the sections "Move a Slide Object" and "Resize a Slide Object" later in this chapter.)

1. Click the **Insert** tab on the Ribbon.

2. Click the **Text Box** button.

3. Click and drag in the slide where you want to place a text box.

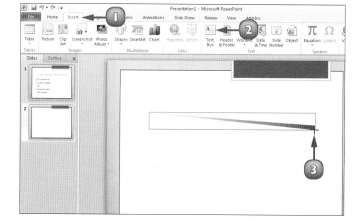

4. Click in the new text box and type your text.

You can click anywhere outside the text box to deselect it.

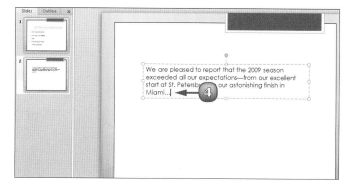

ADD OTHER OBJECTS TO A SLIDE

One way to make your slides more visually appealing is to insert photographs, video clips, tables or charts. When you add an object to a slide, you can control the placement and size of it. In addition to inserting your own picture files into your PowerPoint slides, you can insert clip art, which is artwork supplied by Microsoft. A video clip can play during a slide show presentation.

You can add tables to your slides to organise data in an orderly fashion. Tables use a column-and-row format to present information. Adding an Excel chart to a PowerPoint slide turns numeric data into a visual element that your audience can quickly interpret and understand.

Add a Picture

1. Click the **Insert Picture** icon (🖼) in the slide or on the Insert tab.

   The Insert Picture dialog box opens.

2. Locate and select the picture you want to insert.

3. Click **Insert**.

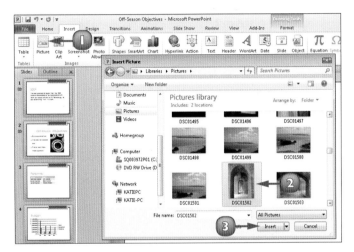

A. *PowerPoint inserts the picture into the slide.*

B. *PowerPoint displays the Picture Tools Format tab on the Ribbon.*

4. To edit the picture (in this example, to change its colour), click the **Format** tab.

5. Click the **Color** button.

6. Choose a colour option.

   PowerPoint updates the image to reflect your edits.

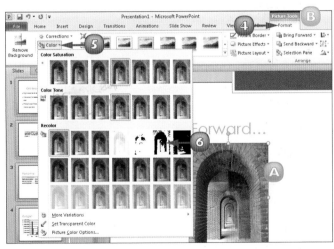

Add a Video Clip

1 Click the **Video** button on the Insert tab.

2 Locate and select the video in the Insert Video dialog box.

3 Click **Insert**.

PowerPoint inserts the clip and displays the Video Tools tabs.

4 Click the **Format** tab to change the video.

5 Click the **Play** button (▶) to play back the clip.

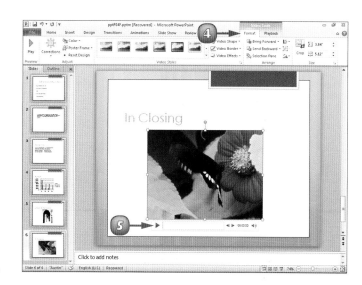

Add a Table

1 Click the **Insert Table** icon (▦) in your slide.

2 Type the number of columns and rows that you want in the table.

3 Click **OK**.

PowerPoint inserts the table and displays the Table Tools tabs.

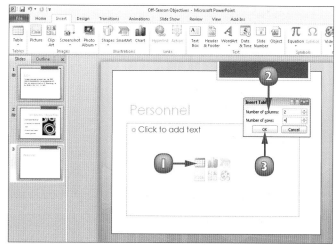

Add a Chart

1 Click the **Chart** button on the Insert tab.

2 Click a chart category and a chart type and click **OK**.

3 Replace the placeholder data with the chart data.

4 Click the **Close** button (✕) to close the Excel window.

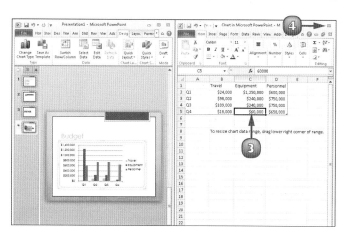

MOVE A SLIDE OBJECT

You can move any slide element, such as a text box, table, chart, picture, video clip or any other element, to reposition it in the slide. (These slide elements are often referred to as *objects*.) For example, you might move a text box to make room for a clip-art object or move a picture to improve the overall appearance of the slide.

One way to move a slide object is to use the standard Office Cut and Paste buttons, discussed in Chapter 2. Another is to drag and drop the object, as discussed in this section.

1 Click the slide object that you want to move to select it.

The ⌖ changes to ⊹.

2 Drag the object to a new location on the slide.

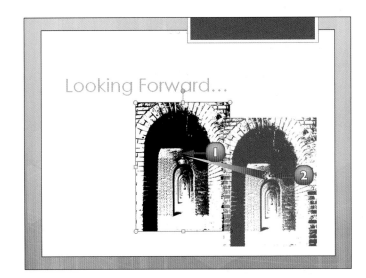

3 Release the mouse button.

Ⓐ *PowerPoint repositions the object.*

4 Click outside the slide object to deselect it.

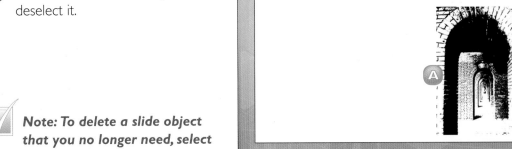

Note: To delete a slide object that you no longer need, select the object and press Delete.

RESIZE A SLIDE OBJECT

After you insert an object, such as a text box, table, chart, picture, video clip or any other element, you may find that you need to make it larger or smaller in order to achieve the desired effect. For example, you might want to resize a text box to make room for more text or resize a picture object to enlarge the artwork. Fortunately, PowerPoint makes it easy to change the size of a slide object. When you select an object in a PowerPoint slide, handles appear around that object; you can use these handles to make the object larger or smaller.

① Click the slide object that you want to resize to select it.

   Ⓐ *PowerPoint surrounds the object box with handles.*

② Position your mouse pointer over a handle.

   The ☖ changes to ☝.

③ Click and drag the handle inward or outward to resize the slide object.

   Drag a corner handle to resize the object's height and width at the same time.

   Drag a side handle to resize the object along only one side.

④ Release the mouse button.

   Ⓑ *PowerPoint resizes the object.*

⑤ Click outside the slide object to deselect it.

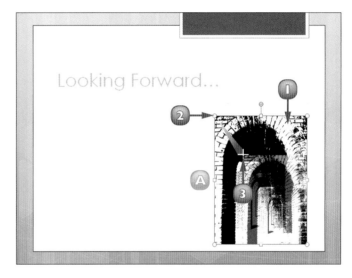

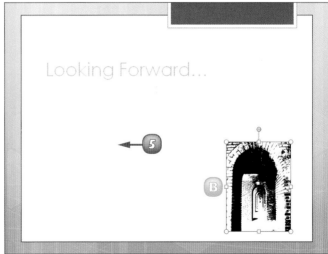

REORGANISE SLIDES

You can change the order of your slides. For example, you may want to move a slide to appear later in the presentation or swap the order of two side-by-side slides. PowerPoint makes it easy to change the slide order in Slide Sorter view or by using the Slides tab in Normal view. (To switch to Slide Sorter view, click the View tab and then click the Slide Sorter button. To switch back to Normal view, click the Normal button in the View tab.) You can move individual slides or move multiple slides at once.

Move Slides in Normal View

1 In Normal view, click the slide that you want to move on the Slides tab.

Note: *You can move multiple slides at once. To do so, press and hold* **Ctrl** *as you click the slides.*

2 Drag the slide to a new location on the tab.

3 Release the mouse button.

A *PowerPoint moves the slide.*

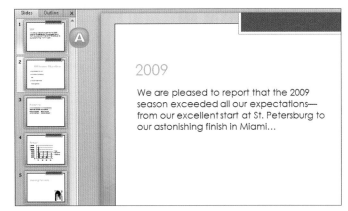

144

Move Slides in Slide Sorter View

① In Slide Sorter view, click the slide that you want to move.

Note: *You can move multiple slides at once. To do so, press and hold* Ctrl *as you click each slide.*

② Drag the slide to a new location in the presentation.

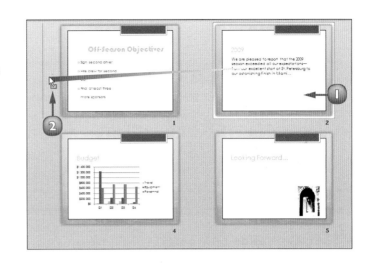

③ Release the mouse button.

Ⓐ *PowerPoint moves the slide.*

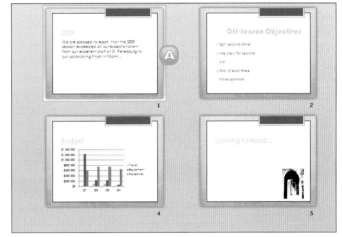

 *If you need to, you can hide a slide. Switch to Slide Sorter view, click the **Slide Show** tab and then click the **Hide Slide** button. The Hide Slide icon (⬚) appears next to the slide in Slide Sorter view. To unhide the slide, repeat these steps.*

 To delete a slide, right-click it in Slide Sorter view or in the Slides tab and choose Delete Slide from the menu that appears.

RECORD NARRATION

Many presentations benefit from narration. One way to provide narration is to simply speak during your presentation. Alternatively, you can use PowerPoint's Record Narration feature to record a narration track to go along with the show (assuming, of course, that your computer has a microphone). That way, you need not be present for your audience to receive the full impact of your presentation. PowerPoint saves the recorded narration along with the presentation file. When you finish recording, an audio icon appears at the bottom of each slide for which you have recorded narration.

① Click the **Slide Show** tab on the Ribbon.

② Click **Record Slide Show**.

The Record Slide Show dialog box appears.

Ⓐ *Make sure the **Narrations and laser pointer** check box is selected.*

③ Click **Start Recording**.

PowerPoint starts the show and you can begin talking into the computer's microphone to record your narration.

Ⓑ *Click ➡ to move to the next slide in the show.*

Ⓒ *Click ▐▐ to pause the recording.*

Ⓓ *Click ↩ to start over on the current slide.*

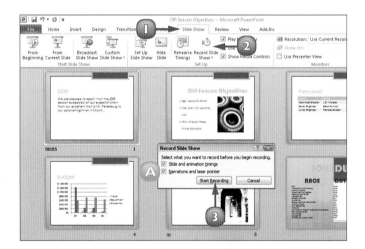

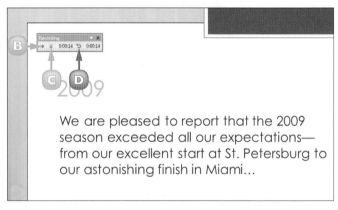

We are pleased to report that the 2009 season exceeded all our expectations— from our excellent start at St. Petersburg to our astonishing finish in Miami...

You can time exactly how long each slide displays during a presentation. PowerPoint saves the timings for use when *you present the slide show to your audience. Click the* Slide Show *tab. Click the* Rehearse Timings *button.*

SET UP A SLIDE SHOW

You can set up how you want your presentation to run. For example, you can specify whether it should loop continuously, be played back in full, be shown without narration or animations and more. If the presentation will be presented by a speaker (rather than, for example, run at a kiosk), you can choose a colour for the pen and laser pointer; the speaker can then use his or her mouse pointer to draw on or point to slides. To set up your slide show, you use the Set Up Show dialog box.

① Click the **Slide Show** tab on the Ribbon.

② Click **Set Up Slide Show**.

The Set Up Show dialog box appears.

③ Set any options that you want to assign to the show.

Ⓐ *The Show Type settings specify how the slide show is presented.*

Ⓑ *The Show Options settings control looping, narration, and animation.*

Ⓒ *The Show Slides settings specify what slides appear in the show.*

Ⓓ *The Advance Slides settings specify how each slide advances.*

Ⓔ *If your system has multiple monitors, you can use the Multiple Monitors settings to specify what monitor to use.*

④ Click **OK**.

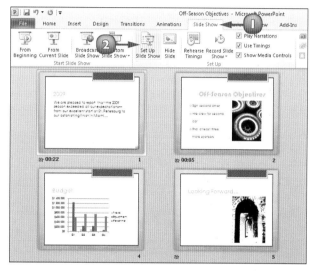

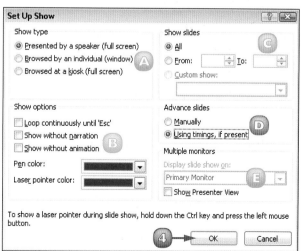

RUN A SLIDE SHOW

You can run a slide show presentation using PowerPoint's Slide Show view. Slide Show view displays full-screen images of your slides. You can advance each slide manually by clicking buttons that appear on-screen; alternatively, you can instruct PowerPoint to advance the slides for you.

To enrich the experience for your audience, you can use PowerPoint's pointer options to draw directly on the screen using the mouse pointer. (You can choose from several pen tools and colours.) For example, you might circle an important sales figure or underline a critical point on a slide. You can end a slide show at any time by pressing Esc.

1 Click the **Slide Show** tab.

2 Click the **From Beginning** button.

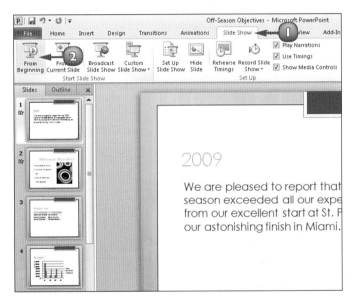

PowerPoint switches to Slide Show mode and displays the first slide.

A *When you move the mouse pointer to the bottom left corner, faint slide show control buttons appear.*

3 Click anywhere in the slide to advance to the next slide or click the **Next** button (➡).

B *To return to a previous slide, you can click the **Previous** button (◀).*

C *To view a menu of slide show commands, click 🗐.*

D *You can pause the show by clicking the* **Pause** *command.*

E *You can end the show early by clicking the* **End Show** *command.*

4 When the slide show is complete, click anywhere on the screen.

PowerPoint closes the presentation.

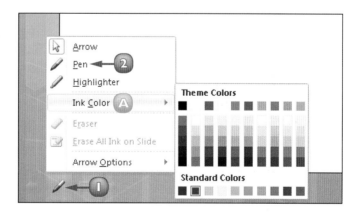

Draw on Slides While Presenting the Show

1 During the slide show, click the **Pen** button (✐).

2 Click a pen style.

A *You can click here to choose a pen colour.*

3 Click and drag to draw on the slide.

To erase your markings, press **E**.

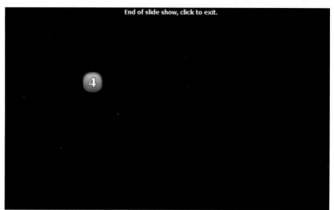

CONTENTS

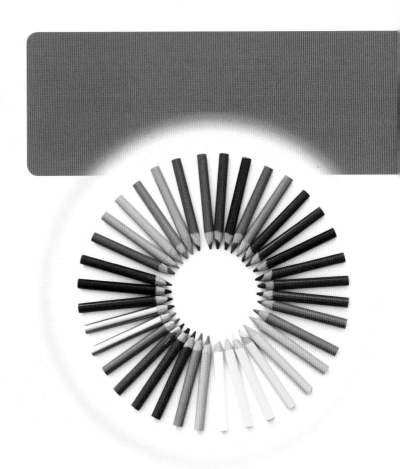

ACCESS

Access is a robust database program you can use to store and manage large quantities of data. You can use Access to manage anything from a home inventory to a database of clients to a giant warehouse of products. Access can help you organise your information into tables, speed up data entry with forms and perform powerful analysis using filters and queries. In this part, you learn how to build and maintain a database file, add tables, create forms, enter data into your database and analyse your data using filters, sorting and queries. You also learn how to run reports on your data.

CREATE A DATABASE BASED ON A TEMPLATE

You can build a new database based on any of the predefined Access templates. For example, the Business category includes templates for creating contact lists, assets, marketing projects and events. You can also log onto the Office Web site to find new templates you can download.

When you create a new database using a template, the database includes pre-built tables and forms, which you can populate with your own data. You control the structure of your database by determining the preset tables and fields that are included in the file.

1. Click the **File** tab.

2. Click **New**.

3. Click **Sample templates**.

   Ⓐ You can also download templates from the Office Web site by clicking a template category under Office.com Templates.

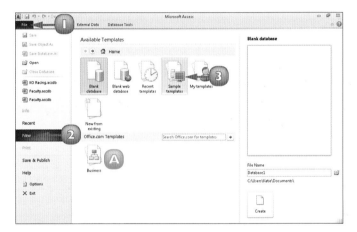

4. Click a template.

5. To change the name of the database, type a new name in the **File Name** field.

6. To change the folder in which the database file will be stored, click the **Browse** button (🖼).

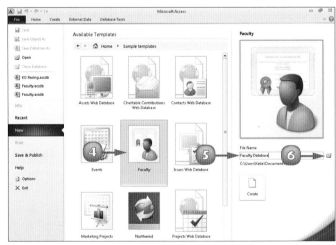

Access launches the File New Database dialog box.

7 Locate and select the folder in which you want to store the database file.

8 Click **OK**.

9 Click **Create**.

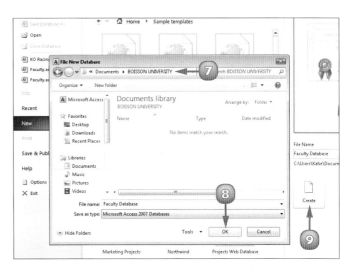

Access creates a new, blank database based on the template you chose and opens a new table, ready for data.

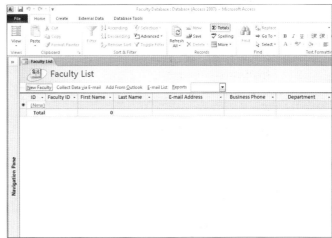

To determine what fields you need in your database, do a little planning. Decide what kinds of information you want to track in your database and what sorts of reports and queries you want to generate to view your data. For best results, use the suggested fields; you can always remove fields that you do not use at a later time. (For help removing fields from a table, see the section "Delete a Field from a Table" later in this chapter.)

CREATE A BLANK DATABASE

If you determine that none of the predefined Access templates suits your purposes, you can create a new, blank database. You can then decide what tables, fields, forms and other database objects your database will include.

When you create a new database file, Access launches the File New Database dialog box and prompts you to assign a name to the file. You also specify the folder and drive in which the database file will be stored.

① Click the **File** tab.

② Click **New**.

③ Click **Blank database**.

④ Type a name for the database in the **File Name** field.

⑤ To change the folder in which the database file will be stored, click the **Browse** button ([icon]).

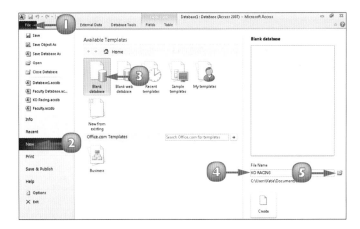

Access launches the File New Database dialog box.

⑥ Locate and select the folder in which you want to store the database file.

⑦ Click **OK**.

8 Click **Create**.

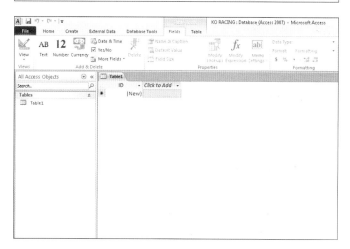

Access creates a new, blank database and opens a new table, ready for data.

You can use the Navigation pane, on the left, to open various database objects. You can collapse the pane to increase the on-screen workspace; simply click the Shutter Bar Open/Close button (<<). Click the button again to expand the pane.

To open an existing database, click the File tab, click Recent and click the database in the Recent Databases list. If the database is not listed in the Recent Databases list, click the File tab, choose Open to launch an Open dialog box, locate and select the database file and click Open.

CREATE A NEW TABLE

Access databases store all data in tables. A *table* is a list of information organised into columns and rows that intersect to form *cells* for holding data. A table might list the names, addresses, phone numbers, company names, titles and e-mail addresses of your clients. Each row in a table is considered a *record*. You can use columns to hold *fields*, which are the individual units of information contained within a record.

If you need to add a table to a database, you can easily do so. All table objects that you create appear listed in the Navigation pane; simply double-click a table object to open it.

1 With your database open in Access, click the **Create** tab.

2 Click the **Table** button.

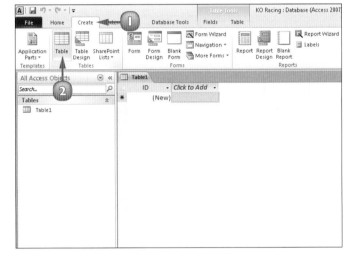

A *Access creates a new table and displays it in Datasheet view.*

Note: *See the "Change Table Views" section to learn more about Datasheet view.*

3 To name a field, click the **Click to Add** link at the top of the field column.

4 Click the type of field you want to add (here, **Text**).

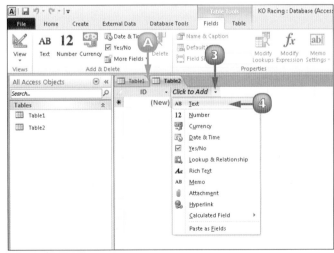

5 Type a name for the field and press **Enter**.

6 Repeat Steps **3** to **5** to create more fields for the table.

7 When you are finished adding fields, close the table by clicking the **Close** button (☒).

Access prompts you to save the table changes.

8 Click **Yes**.

The Save As dialog box appears.

9 Type a name for the table.

10 Click **OK**.

Access lists the table among the database objects in the Navigation pane.

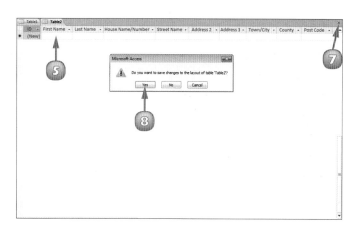

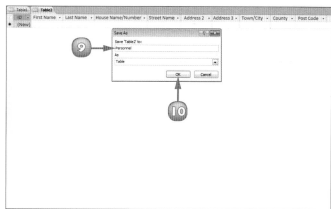

To delete a table, select it in the Navigation pane and press **Delete**. Access asks you to confirm the deletion before permanently removing the table, along with any data that it contains. Before attempting to remove a table, ensure that it does not contain any important data that you need.

You can rename fields in any table. To do so, double-click the field label and type a new name. When you finish, press **Enter**.

CHANGE TABLE VIEWS

You can view your table data using two different view modes: Datasheet view and Design view. In Datasheet view, the table appears as a grid of intersecting columns and rows where you can enter data. In Design view, you can view the skeletal structure of your fields and their properties and modify the design of the table. For example, you can add fields by typing new field names in the Field Name column. You can also change the field names or change the type of data that is allowed within a field, such as text or number data.

Switch to Design View

① Click the **Home** tab on the Ribbon.

② Click the bottom half of the **View** button.

③ Click **Design View**.

Note: *An even quicker way to switch from Datasheet view to Design view is to click the top half of the **View** button.*

Access displays the table in Design view, showing the table's field properties.

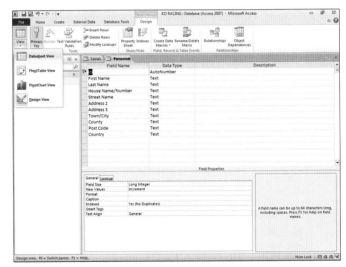

Switch to Datasheet View

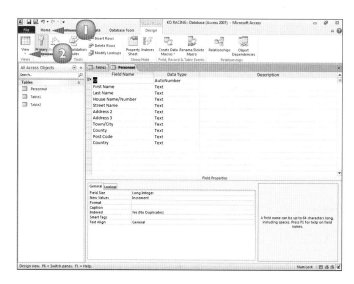

 Click the **Home** tab on the Ribbon.

 Click the bottom half of the **View** button.

 Click **Datasheet View**.

Note: An even quicker way to switch from Design view to Datasheet view is to click the top half of the **View** button.

Access displays the default Datasheet view of the table.

 If you create a PivotTable, you can use PivotTable view to summarise and analyse data by viewing different fields. You can use the PivotChart feature to create a graphical version of a PivotTable and to see various graphical representations of the data. See the Access help files to learn more about the PivotTable and PivotChart features.

 The Field Properties area enables you to change the design of a field, specifying how many characters the field can contain, whether it can be left blank and other properties.

ADD OR MOVE A FIELD IN A TABLE

You can add fields to your table to include more information in your records. For example, you may need to add a separate field to a Contacts table for mobile phone numbers. Alternatively, you may need to add a field to a table that contains a catalogue of products to track each product's availability.

If you built your database from a predefined template, you may find that the order in which fields appear in the table does not suit your needs. If so, you may want to move a field so that it appears before another field to suit the way you type your record data. Fortunately, Access makes it easy to move a field in your table to change how you view and enter record data.

Add a Field

1. Open the table to which you want to add a field in Datasheet view.

2. Click a column header. Access will add the new field to the right of the column you select.

3. Click the **Fields** tab.

4. In the Add & Delete group, click the button for the type of field you want to add (here, **Text**).

   Access adds the new field.

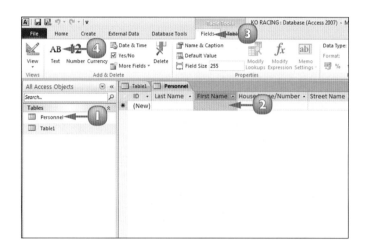

Move a Field

1. In Datasheet view, click the column header for the field you want to move.

2. Drag the column to a new position in the table.

   The ⇧ changes to ⇩.

   (A) A bold vertical line marks the new location of the column.

3. Release the mouse button.

   Access moves the field to the new location.

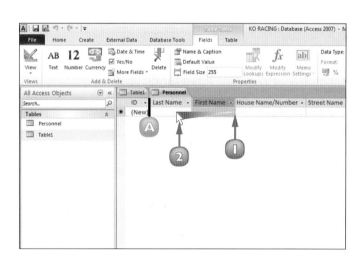

DELETE OR HIDE A FIELD IN A TABLE

You can delete a field that you no longer need in a table. For example, if you are working on a database of employee contact information that contains a Pager field, but your company no longer supports the use of pagers, you might opt to delete that field. When you remove a field, Access permanently removes any data contained within the field for every record in the table.

If your table contains fields that you do not want to view on a regular basis but that you do not want to delete, you can hide them. For example, a table containing a catalogue of products might include a field indicating the country in which the product was manufactured – information that you may not need to view on a regular basis. When you are ready to view the field again, you can easily unhide it.

Delete a Field

1. Open the table that you want to edit in Datasheet view.

2. Click the **Fields** tab.

3. Click the column header for the field you want to remove.

4. Click the **Delete** button.

Access removes the field and any record content for the field from the table.

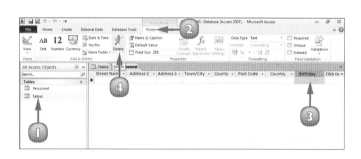

Hide a Field

1. Click the column header for the field you want to hide.

2. Right-click the selection.

3. Click **Hide Fields**.

Access hides the field.

Note: To view the field again, right-click the field next to the hidden field, click **Unhide Fields**, select the column and click **OK**.

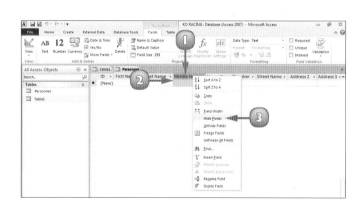

CREATE A FORM

One way to enter data into your database is to type it directly into an Access table. Alternatively, you can create a form based on your table to simplify data entry.

Forms present your table fields in an easy-to-read, fill-in-the-blank format. When you create a form based on a table, Access inserts a field into the form for each field in the table. Forms, which enable you to enter records one at a time, are a great way to speed up data entry, particularly if other users are adding information to your database list.

1 Open the table on which you want to base a form and click the **Create** tab.

2 Click the **Form** button.

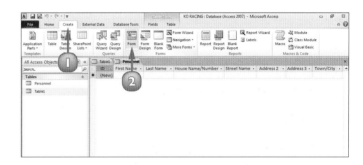

Access creates the form.

3 Click the **Close** button (⊠) to close the form.

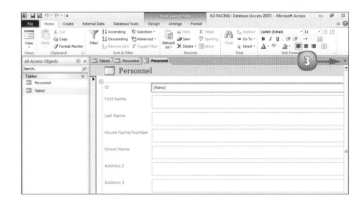

Access prompts you to save your changes.

 Click **Yes**.

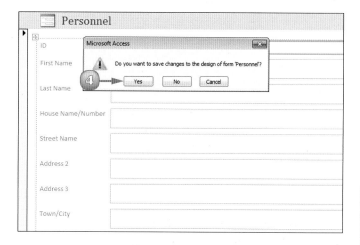

The Save As dialog box appears.

 Type a name for the form.

 Click **OK**.

Access lists the form among the database objects in the Navigation pane.

Note: *After you save a form, you can reopen it by double-clicking it in the Navigation pane.*

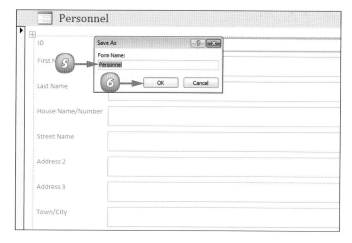

 To delete a form, click it in the Navigation pane. Then press Delete **or click the Delete button on the Home tab. Access asks you to confirm the deletion; click Yes.**

To create a blank form, click the Create tab. Click the Blank Form button. Access opens a blank form and a list containing the fields from all of the tables in the database. To add a field to the form, drag it from the list onto the form. You can populate the form with as many fields as you need.

CHANGE FORM VIEWS

You can view your forms in various ways: Form view, Design view and Layout view. Form view is the default; in this view, you can simply enter data. In Design view, each form object appears as a separate, editable element. For example, in this view, you can edit the box that contains the data and the label that identifies the data. In Layout view, you can rearrange the form controls and adjust their sizes directly on the form. Access makes it easy to switch from Form view to Design view to Layout view and back.

Switch to Design View

1. Click the **Home** tab on the Ribbon.

2. Click the bottom half of the **View** button.

3. Click **Design View**.

   Access displays the form in Design view.

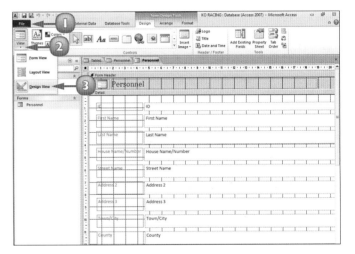

Switch to Layout View

1. Click the **Home** tab on the Ribbon.

2. Click the bottom half of the **View** button.

3. Click **Layout View**.

   Access displays the form in Layout view.

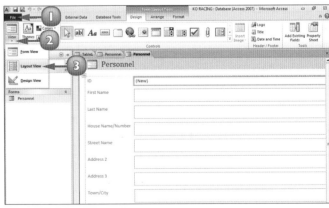

 To return to Form view, click the bottom half of the View button and then click Form View.

MOVE OR DELETE A FIELD IN A FORM

You can move a field to another location on your form. When you select a field for editing, the field label is also selected, making it easy to move both the field and the label at the same time.

You can delete a field that you no longer need in a form. You need to remove both the data box and the field label. Note that removing a form field does not remove the field from the table on which the form is based, or its data.

Although you can move and delete fields in Design view or in Layout view, you might find it easier to make changes to your form in Layout view.

Move a Field

1. Open the form that you want to edit in Layout view.
2. Click the field that you want to move.
3. Click and drag the field to the new location on the form.

   The ↖ changes to ✥.

   Access repositions the field.

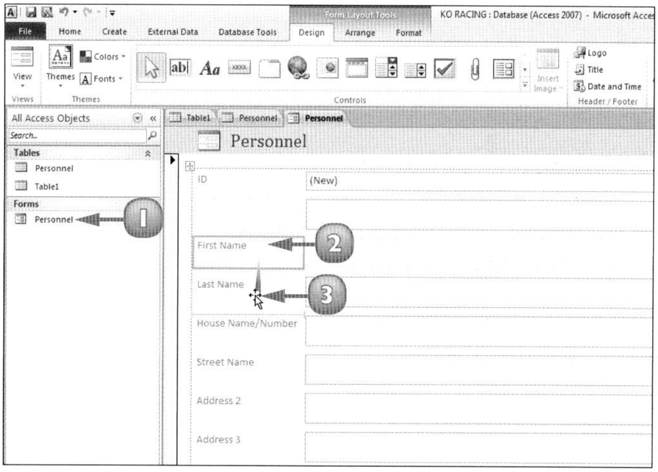

Delete a Field

1. Open the form that you want to edit in Layout view.
2. Click the field that you want to delete.
3. Press Delete or click the **Delete** button on the Home tab.

   Access removes the field and label from the form.

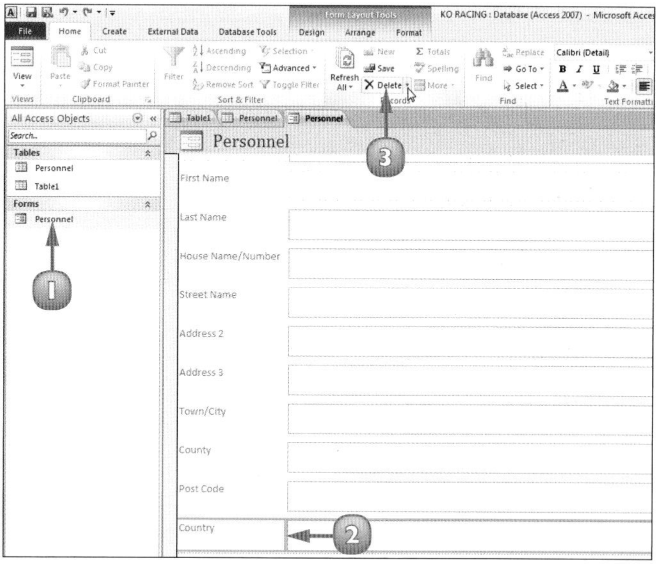

ADD A RECORD TO A TABLE

You build a database by adding records to a table in the database. Any new records that you add appear at the end of the table. After you enter a record in a database table, you can edit it if necessary. You add and edit records in a table in Datasheet view.

As your table grows longer, you can use the navigation buttons on your keyboard to navigate it. You can press **Tab** to move from cell to cell or you can press the keyboard arrow keys. To move backward to a previous cell, press **Shift** + **Tab**.

1 In the Navigation pane, double-click the table to which you want to add a record.

A *Access opens the table, placing the cursor in the first cell of the first blank row.*

B *By default, the first field in each table is an ID field, containing a unique ID number for the record. This value is set automatically.*

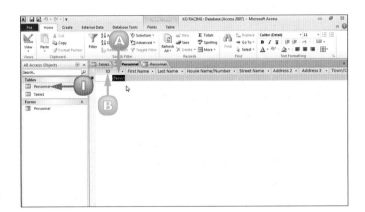

2 Press **Tab**.

Access moves your cursor to the next cell in the row.

3 Type the desired data in the selected cell.

4 Press **Tab**.

5 Repeat Steps **3** and **4** until you have filled the entire row.

6 Press **Enter** or **Tab** to move to the next row, or record.

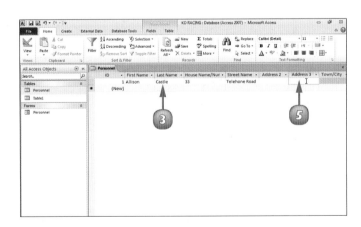

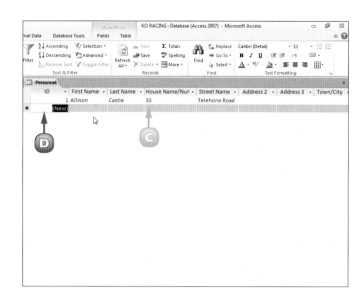

C *Access adds the new record.*

D *Access moves your cursor to the first cell in the next row.*

7 Repeat Steps **2** to **6** to add more records to the table.

E *You can resize a column by dragging the column border left or right.*

F *You can use the scroll bars to view different portions of the table.*

To edit a record, open the table in Datasheet view, click in the cell whose data you want to change, double-click the data to select it and type over the data to replace it.

To delete a record, open the table in Datasheet view. Click the grey box to the left of the record that you want to delete. Right-click the record and then click **Delete Record**. Click **Yes**.

A primary key uniquely identifies each record in a table. For many tables, the primary key is the ID field, which is created automatically and stores a unique number for each record as it is entered into the database

ADD A RECORD TO A FORM

You can use forms to quickly add records to your Access databases. Forms present your record fields in an easy-to-read format. You add records to a form in Form view; this view presents each field in your table as a box that you can use to enter data.

After you enter a record in a form, you can edit it if necessary. For help locating a particular record in the form window in order to edit it, see the next section, "Navigate Records in a Form."

1 In the Navigation pane, double-click the form to which you want to add a record.

A *If the form is not visible in the Navigation pane, click ⊙, choose **Object Type** and locate the desired form under the Forms heading.*

Access opens the form.

2 Click the **Home** tab.

3 Click the **New** button in the Records group.

B *Access opens a blank form, placing the cursor in the first field.*

C *By default, the first field is an ID field, containing a unique ID number for the record. This value is set automatically.*

4 Press `Tab`.

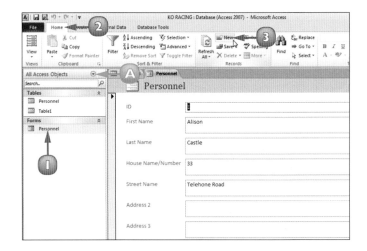

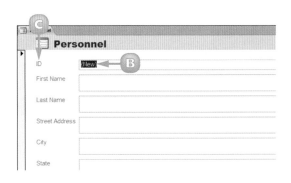

Access moves your cursor to the next field in the form.

⑤ Type the desired data in the selected field.

⑥ Press **Tab**.

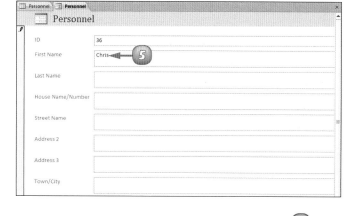

Access moves to the next field in the form.

⑦ Repeat Steps **5** and **6** until you have filled the entire form.

⑧ Press **Enter** or **Tab**.

Access displays another blank record, ready for data.

Ⓓ *To close the form window, you can click the **Close** button (☒).*

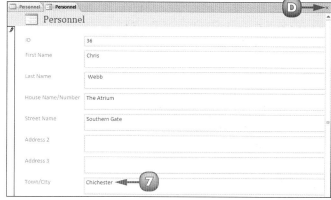

 *You can also create a new record by clicking the **New (Blank) Record** button (⏵⁛) on the form window's navigation bar (located along the bottom of the form).*

 To edit a record, open the form, navigate to the record that you want to change and make your edits directly to the form data. When you save your changes, Access automatically updates the data in the table.

 *To delete a record from a form, open the form and navigate to the record that you want to delete. Click the **Home** tab on the Ribbon. Click the **Delete** button's ▾ and click **Delete Record**. Click **Yes**.*

NAVIGATE RECORDS IN A FORM

You may find it easier to read a record using a form instead of reading it from a large table containing other records. Similarly, editing a record in a form may be easier than editing a record in a table. You can locate records you want to view or edit using the navigation bar that appears along the bottom of the form window. This navigation bar contains buttons for locating and viewing different records in your database. The navigation bar also contains a Search field for locating a specific record. (You learn how to search for a record in a form in the next section.)

① In the Navigation pane, double-click the form whose records you want to navigate.

Note: *If the form is not visible in the Navigation pane, click the* ▼ *along the top of the pane, choose **Object Type** and locate the desired form under the Forms heading.*

Access displays the form.

Ⓐ *The Current Record box indicates what record you are viewing.*

② Click **Previous Record** (◀) or **Next Record** (▶) to move back or forward by one record.

Ⓑ *Access displays the previous or next record in the database.*

Ⓒ *Click **First Record** (◀◀) or **Last Record** (▶▶) to navigate to the first or last record in the table.*

Ⓓ *Click **New (Blank) Record** (▶✳) to start a new, blank record.*

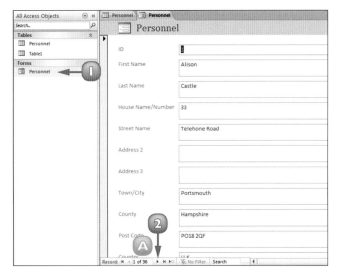

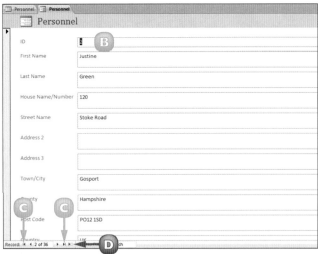

SEARCH FOR A RECORD IN A FORM

As mentioned, you may find it easier to read and edit records in a form than in a large table containing other records.

One way to locate records you want to view or edit is to use the various buttons in the navigation bar, such as the Previous Record button, the Next Record button and so on. (Refer to the preceding section for help using these buttons.) This method can become time-consuming, however, if the form contains many records. An easier approach is to search for the record using Access's search functionality, also accessible from the navigation bar.

1 In the Navigation pane, double-click the form containing the record you want to find.

Note: *If the form is not visible in the Navigation pane, click the* ▼ *along the top of the pane, choose* **Object Type** *and locate the desired form under the Forms heading.*

Access displays the form.

2 Click in the **Search** field.

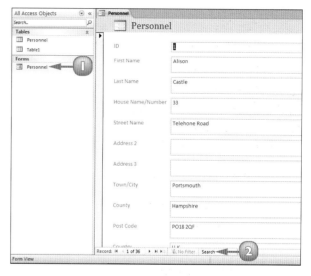

3 Type a keyword that relates to the record you want to find (here, a person's last name).

A As you type, Access displays matching records.

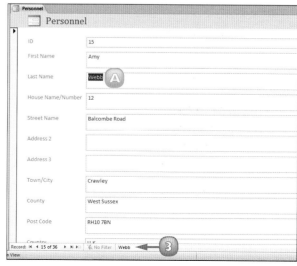

SORT RECORDS

Sorting enables you to arrange your database records in a logical order to match any criteria that you specify. For example, with a contacts database, you might sort the records alphabetically or based on the post (or ZIP) code. You can sort in ascending order or descending order. For example, if you are sorting alphabetically, you can sort from A to Z (ascending) or from Z to A (descending).

You can sort records in a table or you can use a form to sort records. In this section, you learn how to do both.

Sort a Table

1. Open the table you want to sort.

2. Position your mouse pointer over the column header for the field by which you want to sort (the mouse pointer changes to ↓) and click.

3. Click the **Home** tab on the Ribbon.

4. Click a sort button.

Click **Ascending** to sort the records in ascending order.

Click **Descending** to sort the records in descending order.

Access sorts the table records based on the field you choose.

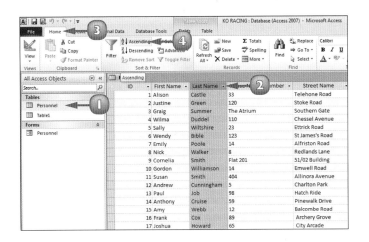

A. This example sorts the records alphabetically by last name in ascending order.

B. In the prompt box that appears when you close the table, you can click **Yes** to make the sort permanent or **No** to leave the original order intact.

172

Sort Using a Form

1 Open the form you want to sort.

2 Click in the field by which you want to sort.

3 Click the **Home** tab on the Ribbon.

4 Click a sort button.

Click **Ascending** to sort the records in ascending order.

Click **Descending** to sort the records in descending order.

Access sorts the table records based on the field you choose.

A This example sorts the records alphabetically by last name in ascending order.

B You can use the navigation buttons to view the sorted records.

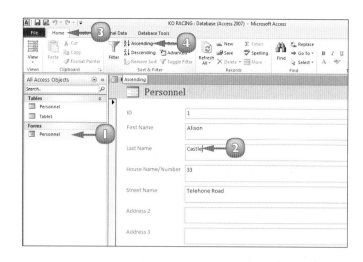

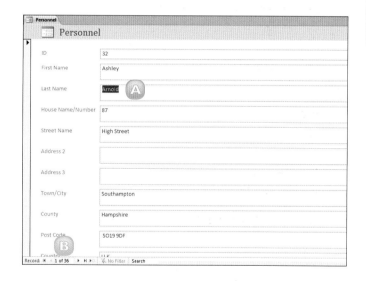

 If you perform a sort on a field for which some records are missing data, those records are included in the sort. Records with empty fields are sorted first when you perform an ascending sort and last with a descending sort.

 To remove a sort order, click the Remove Sort button in the Sort & Filter group on the Home tab. This returns the table to its original sort order. You can also use this technique to remove a sort from a query or report. (Queries and reports are covered later in this chapter.)

FILTER RECORDS

You can use an Access filter to view only records that meet criteria you set. For example, you may want to view all clients buying a particular product, anyone in a contacts database who has a birthday in June or all products within a particular category. You can also filter by exclusion — that is, filter out records that do not contain the search criteria that you specify.

You can apply a simple filter on one field in your database using the Selection tool or you can filter several fields using the Filter by Form command.

Apply a Simple Filter

1 Open the form you want to filter.

2 Click in the field by which you want to filter.

3 Click the **Home** tab on the Ribbon.

4 Click the **Selection** button.

5 Click a criterion.

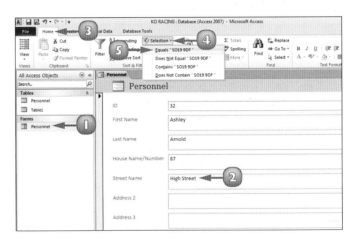

Access filters the records.

A *In this example, Access finds two records matching the filter criterion.*

B *You can use the navigation buttons to view the filtered records.*

C *To undo a filter, click the* **Toggle Filter** *button.*

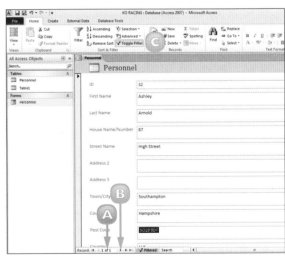

Filter by Form

1. Open the form you want to filter.

2. Click the **Home** tab on the Ribbon.

3. Click the **Advanced** button.

4. Click **Filter By Form**.

   A blank form appears.

5. Click in the field by which you want to filter.

6. Click the ▼ that appears and choose a criterion.

7. Repeat Steps **5** and **6** to add more criteria to the filter.

    You can set OR criteria using the tabs at the bottom of the form.

8. Click the **Toggle Filter** button.

   Access filters the records.

   To remove the filter, you can click the **Toggle Filter** button again.

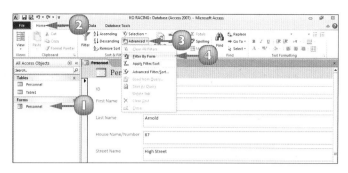

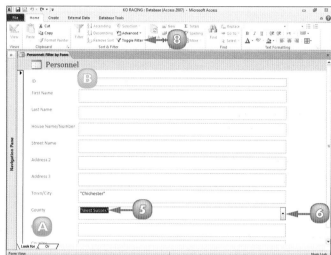

 To filter by exclusion, click in the form field on which you want to filter. Click the Selection button on the Home tab and then click an exclusion option. Access filters out any records that do not contain the data found in the field that you selected.

 OR criteria enable you to display records that match one set of criteria or another. For example, you might set up your filter to display only those records with the value Jones OR the value Smith in the Last Name field.

USE CONDITIONAL FORMATTING

You can use Access's Conditional Formatting tool to apply certain formatting attributes, such as bold text or a fill colour, to data in a form when the data meets a specified condition. For example, if your database tracks weekly sales, you might set up Access's Conditional Formatting feature to alert you if sales figures fall below what is required for you to break even.

You apply conditional formatting by creating a rule, which specifies the criteria that the value in a field must meet. Values that meet the criteria are formatted using settings you specify.

1 Open the form to which you want to apply conditional formatting in Layout view.

2 Click the field to which you want to apply conditional formatting.

3 Click the **Format** tab.

4 Click the **Conditional Formatting** button.

The Conditional Formatting Rules Manager dialog box opens.

5 Click the **New Rule** button.

The New Formatting Rule dialog box opens.

6 Set the criteria you want to use to apply conditional formatting.

7 Specify how values that meet your criteria should be formatted.

8 Click **OK**.

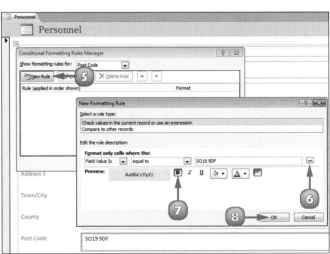

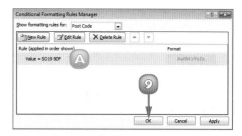

A *Access creates a rule based on the criteria you set.*

9 Click **OK**.

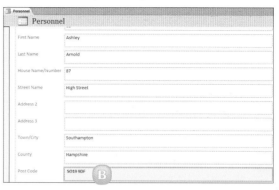

B *Access applies the conditional formatting.*

Remove Conditional Formatting

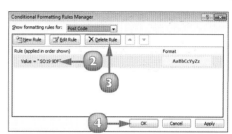

1 Open the Conditional Formatting Rules Manager dialog box. (To open this dialog box, follow Steps **1** to **4** on the previous page.)

2 Click the conditional formatting rule you want to remove.

3 Click the **Delete Rule** button.

4 Click **OK**.

Access removes the conditional formatting.

PERFORM A SIMPLE QUERY

You can use a query to extract information that you want to view in a database. Queries are especially useful when you want to glean data from multiple tables.

Queries are similar to filters but offer you greater control when it comes to viewing records. You can use the Query Wizard to help you select what fields you want to include in the analysis. There are several types of Query Wizard. These include Simple, which is covered here; Crosstab, to display information in a spreadsheet-like format; Find Duplicates, to find records with duplicate field values; and Find Unmatched, to find records in one table with no related records in another table.

Create a Query

1. Open the table or form for which you want to perform a query.

2. Click the **Create** tab on the Ribbon.

3. Click the **Query Wizard** button.

   A New Query dialog box appears.

4. Click **Simple Query Wizard**.

5. Click **OK**.

   The Simple Query Wizard opens.

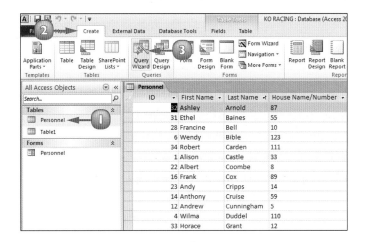

6. Click the **Tables/Queries** ▼ and choose the table on which you want to base the query.

7. In the Available Fields list, click a field to include in the query.

8. Click the **Add** button (▶).

   A. *The field is added to the Selected Fields list.*

9. Repeat Steps **7** and **8** to add more fields to your query.

10. Click **Next.**

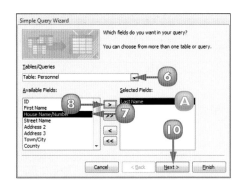

178

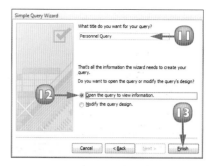

(11) Type a name for the query.

(12) Click the **Open the query to view information** radio button.

(13) Click **Finish**.

A query datasheet appears, listing the fields.

Add Criteria to the Query

(1) Double-click the query in the Navigation pane to open it.

Note: *If it is not visible, click the ▼ at the top of the pane, choose* **Object Type** *and locate the query under the Queries heading.*

(2) Click the **View** button to switch to Design view.

(3) Click in the **Criteria** field and type the data that you want to view.

(4) Click the **View** button again to switch back to Datasheet view to see the results.

The table shows only the records matching the criteria.

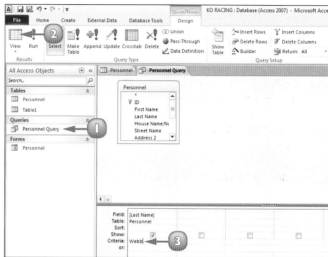

✓ *You can add another table to the query. Switch to Design view, click the Design tab on the Ribbon and then click the Show Table button. This opens the Show Table dialog box, where you can add another table to the query and choose from among the available fields to customise the query.*

✓ *You can use the sorting and filtering features to further define your query results.*

CREATE A REPORT

You can use Access to create a report based on one or more database tables. This can be a simple report, which contains all the fields in a single table, or a custom report, which can contain data from multiple tables in a database. (Note that to use fields from two or more tables, the tables must have a defined relationship.)

To create a custom report, you can use the Report Wizard; it guides you through all the steps necessary to turn complex database data into an easy-to-read report.

Create a Simple Report

① Open the table for which you want to create a simple report.

② Click the **Create** tab on the Ribbon.

③ Click the **Report** button.

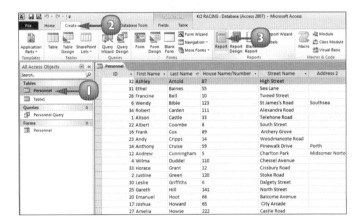

Access creates a simple report based on the table you selected.

 Table relationships enable you to combine related information for analysis. For example, you might define a relationship between a table containing customer contact information and a table containing customer orders. With that table relationship defined, you could perform a query, for example, to locate all customers who have ordered the same product. To define table relationships, click the Database Tools tab in the Ribbon and then click Relationships. (If you created your database from a template, certain relationships are predefined.)

180

Create a Custom Report

① Open a table you want to include in a custom report.

② Click the **Create** tab.

③ Click the **Report Wizard** button.

The Report Wizard opens.

④ Click the **Tables/Queries** ▾ and choose a table you want to include in the report.

⑤ Under Available Fields, click a field that you want to include in the report.

⑥ Click the **Add** button (>).

Ⓐ *The field is added to the Selected Fields list.*

⑦ Repeat Steps **5** and **6** to add more fields.

⑧ Click **Next**.

⑨ Click the field you want to use to group the data.

⑩ Click the **Add** button (>).

Ⓑ *A preview of the grouping appears here.*

⑪ Click **Next**.

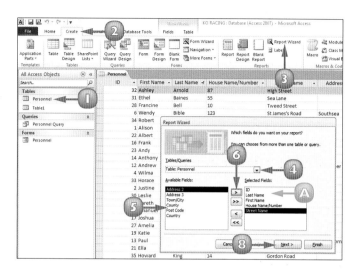

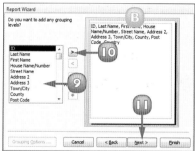

 You can remove a field from the report in the Wizard by clicking the Back button until you reach the wizard's first screen. Then click the field you want to remove in the Selected Fields *list and click the Remove button (<). To remove all the fields, click the Remove All button (<<).*

continued ➡

CREATE A REPORT (continued)

As the Report Wizard guides you through the steps for building a report, you are asked to decide upon a sort order. You can sort records by up to four fields, in ascending or descending order. The wizard also prompts you to select a layout for the report. Options include Stepped, Block and Outline, in either portrait or landscape mode. (Note that you can change other design aspects of the report by opening it in Design view.) After you create the report, you can print it.

12 To sort your data, click the first ▾ and click the field by which you want to sort.

You can add more sort fields as needed.

Note: Fields are sorted in ascending order by default. Click the **Ascending** button to toggle to descending order.

13 Click **Next**.

14 Click a layout option.

c You can set the page orientation for a report using these options.

15 Click **Next**.

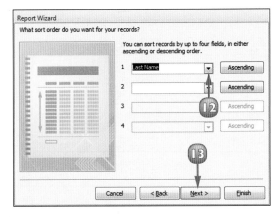

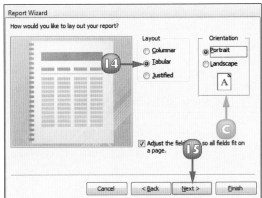

 Type a name for the report.

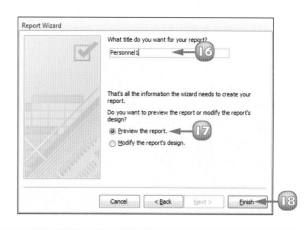

Click the **Preview the report** radio button.

Click **Finish**.

 Access creates the report and displays it in Print Preview mode.

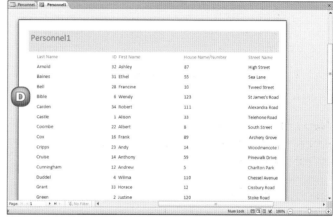

You can further customise a report using Design view. You can change the formatting of fields, move fields around and more. You can even apply conditional formatting to the report by clicking the **Conditional Formatting** button in the Format tab. (For more about conditional formatting, refer to the section "Use Conditional Formatting" earlier in this chapter.)

To print a report from Print Preview view, click the Print Preview tab and click the Print button. Alternatively, click the File button and click Print to open the Print dialog box, where you can select various printing options.

CONTENTS

VI

OUTLOOK

Outlook is a personal information manager for the computer desktop. You can use Outlook's Calendar component to manage appointments in your calendar; its Contacts component to keep track of contacts; its Tasks component to organise lists of tasks you need to complete; its Mail component to send and receive e-mail messages; and more. You can perform a wide variety of everyday tasks from the Outlook window. In this part, you learn how to put Outlook to work for you using each of the major components to manage everyday tasks.

VIEW OUTLOOK COMPONENTS

You can use Outlook to manage everyday tasks. Outlook works much like a personal organiser, with components for performing certain tasks: Mail, Calendar, Contacts and Tasks.

The Outlook Mail component enables you to send and receive e-mail messages. The Outlook Calendar component enables you to keep track of appointments. The Outlook Contacts component enables you to maintain a database of your contacts. The Outlook Tasks component enables you to keep a to-do list. In addition, Outlook features a To-Do Bar to help you stay organised at a glance.

You can easily switch between components, depending on the task that you want to perform.

1 Click the **Calendar** button in the Navigation pane.

A *You can use the To-Do Bar to see your daily items at a glance.*

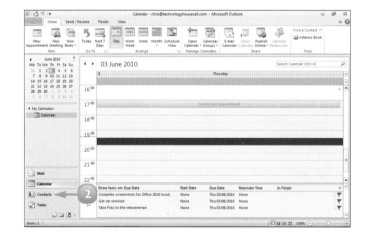

Outlook displays the Calendar component.

2 Click the **Contacts** button in the Navigation pane.

Outlook displays the Contacts component.

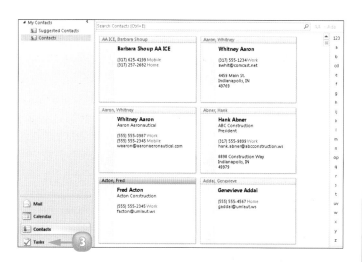

③ Click the **Tasks** button in the Navigation pane.

Outlook displays the Tasks component.

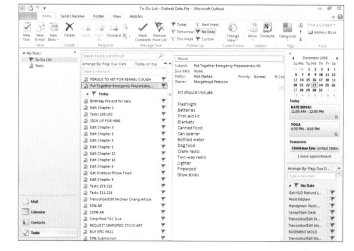

By default, Outlook opens the Mail component's Inbox folder when you start the program. To start with a different Mail folder or another component, such as Calendar, click the File tab, click Options and click Advanced. Under Outlook Start and Exit, click the Browse button. Then click the component or Mail folder that you want to set as the default component in the Select Folder dialog box and click OK in both dialog boxes to close them.

SCHEDULE AN APPOINTMENT

You can use Outlook's Calendar component to keep track of your schedule. When you add a new appointment to the Calendar, you fill out details such as the name of the person with whom you are meeting, the location of the appointment, the date of the appointment and the start and end times of the appointment. You can also enter notes about the appointment, as well as set up Outlook to remind you of the appointment. When you set a reminder, Outlook displays a prompt box at the designated time to remind you about the appointment (assuming, of course, that Outlook is running).

① Click the **Calendar** button in the Navigation pane to open the Calendar component.

② Click the date for which you want to set an appointment.

Ⓐ *Click the Date Navigator's arrow buttons to choose a different month.*

③ Double-click the time slot for the appointment that you want to set.

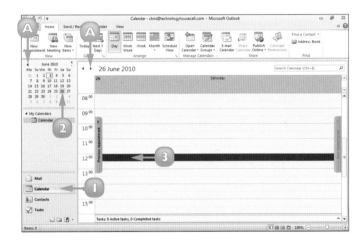

Outlook opens the Appointment window, at the Appointment tab.

④ Type a name for the appointment.

Ⓑ *Outlook adds the name to the window's title.*

⑤ Type a location for the appointment.

⑥ Click the **End time** ▼ and set an end time for the appointment.

Ⓒ *If you did not select the correct time slot in Step **3**, you can click the **Start time** ▼ and click a start time.*

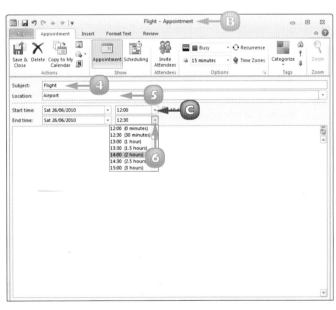

Outlook automatically sets a
reminder for the appointment.

D *You can click the* ☑ *to
change the reminder setting.*

E *You can type any notes about
the appointment here.*

7 Click the **Save & Close** button.

F *Outlook displays the
appointment in the Calendar.*

To view the appointment details
or make changes, you can double-
click the appointment to reopen
the Appointment window.

G *The days on which you have
appointments scheduled
appear bold in the Date
Navigator.*

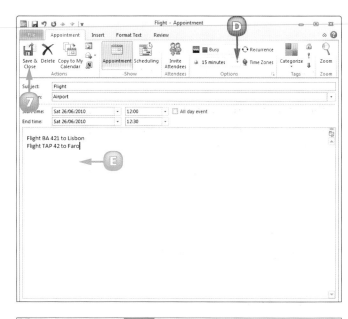

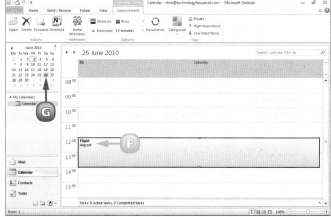

 **You can set up a recurring
appointment. On the
Appointment tab, click the
Recurrence button. In the
Appointment Recurrence
dialog box, select the
recurrence pattern and a range
(if the appointments only
occur for a set period). Click
OK. Recurring appointments
are indicated on the Calendar
by a recurrence icon ().**

**Click the Categorize button
to assign categories to your
appointments. For example,
you might categorise all work
appointments as blue and all
non-work appointments as red.**

SCHEDULE AN EVENT

If you need to track an activity that lasts the entire day or spans several days, such as an anniversary or a conference, you can schedule the activity as an event. Events appear as banners at the top of the scheduled date.

Scheduling an event is similar to scheduling a regular appointment. As with scheduling a regular appointment, you enter a name for the event, specify a location and enter notes about the event as needed. In addition to scheduling events, you can schedule meetings. (For more information, see the tip at the end of this section.)

① Click the **Home** tab.

② Click the **New Items** button.

③ Click **All Day Event**..

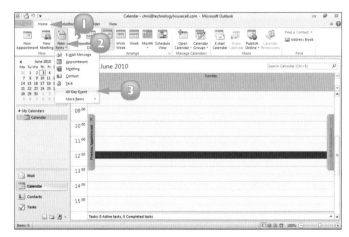

Outlook displays the Event window, which looks the same as the Appointment window.

④ Type a subject for the event.

Ⓐ *Outlook adds the subject to the window's title.*

⑤ Type a location for the event, if applicable.

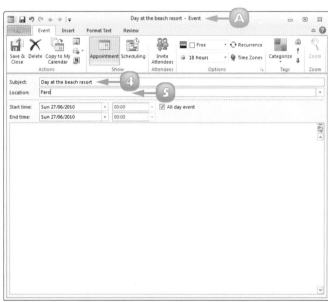

6 Enter the event's date in the **Start time** and **End time** fields.

B *You can click each field's* ▼ *to choose the date from a pop-up calendar.*

7 Click the **Save & Close** button.

C *Outlook displays the event as a banner in the Calendar for the date of the event.*

Note: *To edit an event, you can double-click the event banner and make your changes in the appointment window that opens.*

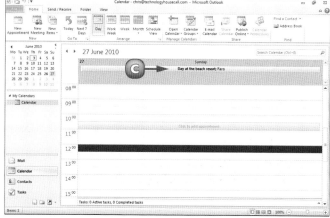

 To publish a calendar online, click the Home tab, click Publish Online and then click Publish to Office.com. Outlook prompts you to register with Office Online before launching a wizard to step you through the publication process. After your calendar is published, Outlook prompts you to invite others to view it; follow the on-screen instructions.

 To schedule meetings with other users, click the Home tab and click the New Meeting button to open a Meeting window; then enter the requested information.

CREATE A NEW CONTACT

You can use Outlook's Contacts component to maintain contact information for people with whom you want to remain in touch, such as family members, co-workers and clients. Using Outlook Contacts, you can keep track of information about your contacts such as their home address, their business address, their e-mail address, their home phone number, their work phone number, their mobile number and their fax number. You can also enter notes about a contact.

If you use a different program to keep track of your contacts, you may be able to import that information into Outlook. For more information, see the tip at the end of this section.

① Click the **Contacts** button in the Navigation pane to open the Contacts component.

② Click the **New Contact** button.

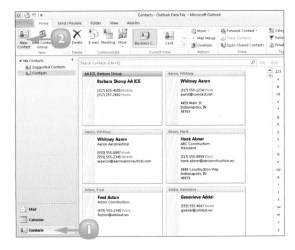

Outlook opens a Contact window.

③ Fill in the contact's information.

You can press `Tab` to move from field to field.

④ Click the **Show** button.

⑤ Click the **Details** button.

⑥ Fill in additional information about the contact, as needed.

⑦ Click the **Save & Close** button.

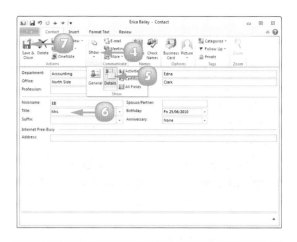

Outlook saves the information and displays the contact in the Contacts list.

To edit contact details, you can double-click the contact to reopen the Contact window.

 *To import a list of contacts from another program, first export the contacts from that program to a file. Click the **File** tab, click **Open** and click **Import** to open the Import and Export Wizard, which steps you through the import process.*

 One way to send an e-mail to a contact is to right-click the contact, click Create and then click E-mail. Outlook opens a Message window with the contact's e-mail address in the To field; add a subject, type your message text and click Send.

CREATE A NEW TASK

You can use Outlook's Tasks component to keep track of things that you need to do, such as a daily list of activities or project steps that you need to complete. You can assign a due date to each task, as well as prioritise and categorise tasks. You can even use Outlook Tasks to assign tasks to other people.

Outlook's Notes component allows you to create notes for yourself, much like an electronic version of yellow sticky notes. You can attach Outlook Notes to other items in Outlook, such as appointments or e-mail messages, as well as drag them from the Outlook window onto the Windows desktop for easy viewing.

① Click the **Tasks** button in the Navigation pane to open the Tasks component.

② Click the **New Task** button.

Outlook displays a Task window.

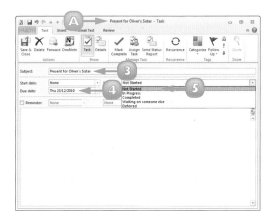

③ Type a subject for the task.

Ⓐ *Outlook adds the subject to the window's title.*

④ Enter a due date for the task.

⑤ Click the **Status** ▾ and click a progress option.

⑥ Type a note or details about the task here.

Ⓑ *You can set a priority level for the task using the* ***Priority*** ▾*.*

Ⓒ *To set a completion amount, you can click the* **% Complete** ▴▾*.*

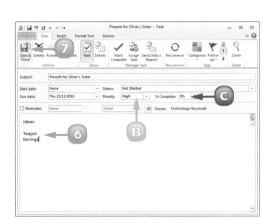

⑦ Click the **Save & Close** button.

D *Outlook displays the task in the Tasks list.*

To view the task details again or make changes, you can double-click the task to reopen the Task window.

E *To change your view of tasks in the Tasks list, you can click the **Change View** button and choose a view option from the menu that appears.*

Add a Note

① Click the **Notes** button (▢) in the Navigation pane to open the Notes component.

② Click the **New Note** button.

Outlook displays a yellow note.

③ Type your note text.

④ When you finish, click the note's **Close** button (▢).

Outlook adds the note to the Notes list.

To view the note again or to make changes, you can double-click the note to reopen it.

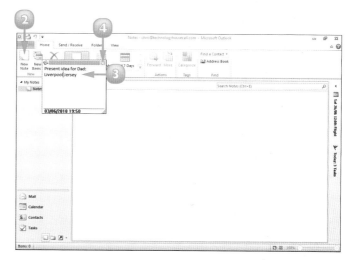

195

COMPOSE AND SEND A MESSAGE

You can use Outlook to compose and send e-mail messages. When you compose a message in Outlook, you designate the e-mail address of the message recipient (or recipients) and type your message text. You can also give the message a subject title to indicate to recipients what the message is about. Although you can compose a message offline, you must log on to your Internet connection to send a message. If you do not have time to finish composing your message during your current work session, you can save the message as a draft for access at a later time instead of sending it.

① Click the **Mail** button in the Navigation pane to open the Mail component.

② Click the **Home** tab.

③ Click the **New E-mail** button.

Outlook opens an untitled message window.

④ Type the recipient's e-mail address.

Ⓐ *If the e-mail address is already in your Address Book, you can click the **To** button and select the recipient's name.*

If you enter more than one e-mail address, you must separate them with a semicolon (;) and a space.

⑤ Type a subject title for the message.

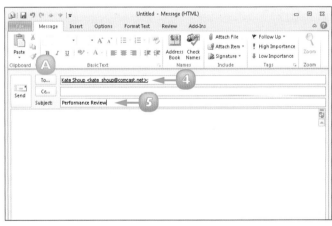

 Type the message text.

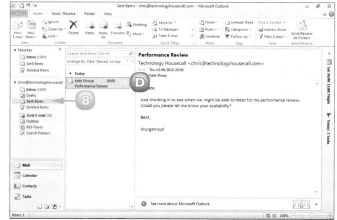 You can use Outlook's formatting buttons to change the appearance of your message text.

To set a priority level for the message, you can click **High Importance** or **Low Importance**.

Note: By default, the message priority level is Normal.

 Click **Send**.

Outlook sends the e-mail message.

Note: You must be connected to the Internet to send the message.

Messages you have sent are stored in the Sent Items folder.

Click the **Sent Items** folder in the Navigation pane.

The message you sent appears in the Item list.

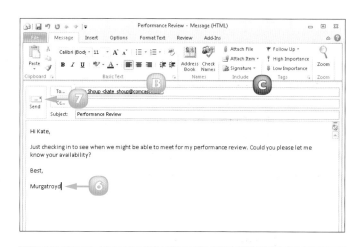

 To save a message as a draft, click the message window's ☒ button and click Yes when prompted to save the message. Outlook saves the message in the Drafts folder. When you are ready to continue composing your message, click the Drafts folder in the Folders list and double-click the saved message to open it.

You can use the Cc or Bcc fields to copy or blind carbon copy the message to another recipient. Either type his or her e-mail address directly in the field or click the Cc or Bcc button to select it from your contacts.

SEND A FILE ATTACHMENT

You can send files stored on your computer to other e-mail recipients. For example, you might send an Excel worksheet or Word document to a work colleague or send a digital photo of your child's birthday to a relative. Assuming that the recipient's computer has the necessary software installed, that person can open and view the file on his or her own system.

Note that some e-mail systems are not set up to handle large file attachments. If you are sending a large attachment, check with the recipient to see if his or her system can handle it.

1 Create a new e-mail message, entering the recipient's e-mail address, a subject title and the message text.

2 Click the **Message** tab.

3 Click the **Attach File** button.

The Insert File dialog box appears.

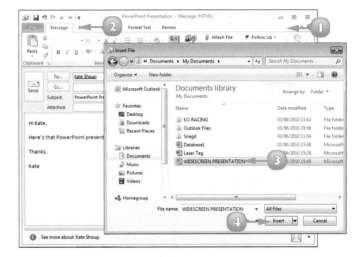

4 Locate and select the file you want to send.

5 Click **Insert**.

A Outlook adds the file attachment to the message and displays the filename and the file size.

6 Click **Send**.

Outlook sends the e-mail message and attachment.

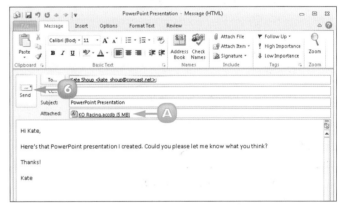

READ AN INCOMING MESSAGE

You can use Outlook's Mail feature to access your e-mail account, download new e-mail messages that others have sent you and view e-mail messages on-screen. You can view a message in a separate message window or in the Reading pane. If the Reading pane is not visible, click the **View** tab, click **Reading Pane** and choose a display option from the list that appears.

You can also view any files attached to the messages you receive (although you should never open a file unless you trust the person who sent it). Note that in order to receive e-mail messages, you must be connected to the Internet.

1 Click the **Send/Receive** tab.

2 Click **Send/Receive All Folders**.

Outlook accesses your e-mail account and downloads any new messages.

3 If the Inbox is not shown, you can click the **Inbox** folder.

4 Click a message in the Item list.

Ⓐ The contents of the message are shown in the Reading pane.

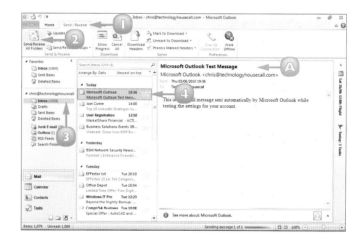

5 Double-click a message in the Item list.

Ⓑ The message opens in a message window.

Note: If the message contains a file attachment, double-click it to open it. A warning dialog box appears; click **Open** to open and display the file in the appropriate program or click **Save** to save the attachment.

REPLY TO OR FORWARD A MESSAGE

You can reply to an e-mail message by sending a return message to the original sender. For example, if you receive an e-mail message containing a question, you can reply to that e-mail with your answer. When you reply to an e-mail, the original sender's name is added to the message's To field.

You can also forward the message to another recipient. For example, you might forward a message that you receive from one co-worker to another co-worker who will find its contents useful. Note that you must be connected to the Internet in order to send replies or forward e-mail messages.

Reply To a Message

① Open the message to which you want to reply.

② Click the **Reply** button to reply to the original sender.

    Ⓐ *To reply to the sender as well as to everyone else who received the original message, you can click the **Reply All** button.*

    Ⓑ *The original sender's address appears in the To field.*

③ Type your reply.

④ Click **Send**.

    Outlook sends the e-mail message.

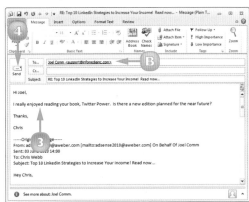

Forward a Message

 Open the message that you want to forward.

② Click the **Forward** button on the Message tab.

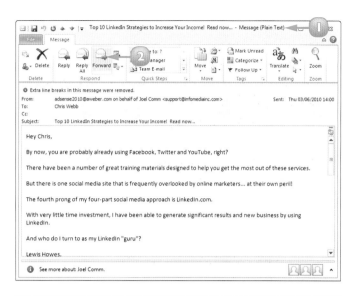

③ Enter the recipient's e-mail address in the To field.

④ Type any message that you want to add to the forwarded e-mail.

⑤ Click **Send**.

Outlook forwards the e-mail message.

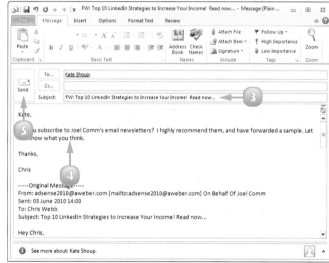

By default, Outlook retains the original message when you click the Reply or Reply All button. To turn off this feature, click the File tab and then click Options. In the Outlook Options dialog box, click Mail. Under Replies and Forwards, click the When replying to a message ▾ and click Do not include original message. Click OK.

Suppose you receive an e-mail message from someone and you do not have a record for that individual in Outlook Contacts. Fortunately, Outlook makes it easy to add the contact information of the sender of any message you receive to your Outlook Contacts, directly from the message itself. Once the person has been added to Outlook Contacts, if you want to send a new message to that person at a later time, you can click the To button in the message window and choose his or her name from the Select Names: Contacts dialog box.

1 Open the message whose sender you want to add to your Outlook Contacts.

2 Right-click the sender's name.

3 Click **Add to Outlook Contacts**.

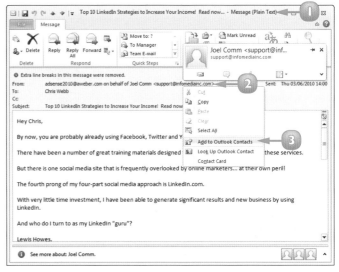

The Contact window opens with the sender's name and e-mail address already filled in.

Ⓐ *You can add additional information as needed.*

4 Click **Save & Close**.

Outlook saves the contact information.

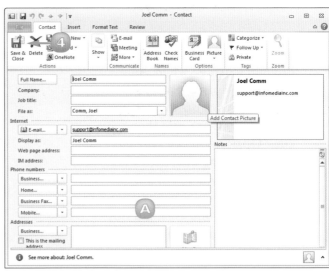

202

DELETE A MESSAGE

As you receive more and more e-mail messages, you may find it difficult to keep your Inbox and other Outlook folders organised. One way to eliminate clutter and keep things manageable is to delete messages you no longer need from your Inbox and other Outlook folders.

Note that when you delete a message from your Inbox or any other Outlook folder, Outlook does not remove it from your system. Rather, it moves it to the Deleted Items folder. To permanently remove deleted messages from your system, thereby maximising your computer's storage capacity, you should purge the Deleted Items folder on a regular basis.

① Locate and select the message that you want to delete.

② Press **Delete** or click the **Delete** button on the Home tab.

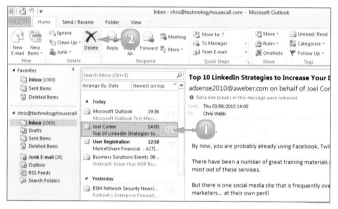

Outlook deletes the message from the Inbox and adds it to the Deleted Items folder.

Ⓐ *You can click the **Deleted Items** folder to view the message that you deleted.*

Ⓑ *To empty the Deleted Items folder, click the **Deleted Items** folder, click the **Folder** tab and click **Empty Folder**.*

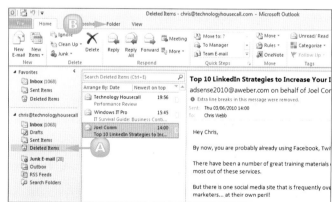

VIEW CONVERSATIONS

In Outlook 2010 Conversation view, you can group messages that are within the same thread, or conversation, in the Item list. This makes your Item list easier to navigate by compressing all related messages, including messages that you have sent as replies or forwarded to others, under a single heading.

As various people contribute to an e-mail conversation, redundant messages may begin to appear in your Inbox. You can use Outlook's Clean Up feature to move redundant messages to the Deleted Items folder. If you have been included in a conversation that is of no relevance to you, you can instruct Outlook to ignore the conversation and move all messages in that conversation to the Deleted Items folder.

① Click the **View** tab.

② Click the **Conversations** button in the Arrangement group.

③ Click **Show Messages in Conversations**.

Ⓐ *Outlook organises your message by conversation.*

④ Click the conversation heading.

⑤ Click the ▷ to expand the conversation.

Outlook expands the conversation, displaying all the related messages.

⑥ Click the ◢ to compress the conversation.

Outlook compresses the conversation, displaying only the conversation heading.

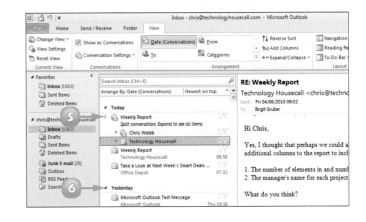

Clean Up a Conversation

① Click a message in the conversation you want to clean up.

② Click the **Home** tab.

③ Click the **Clean Up** button in the Delete group.

④ Click **Clean Up Conversation**.

The Clean Up Conversation dialog box opens.

⑤ Click **Clean Up**.

Outlook removes redundant messages from the conversation.

Messages are placed in the Deleted Items folder.

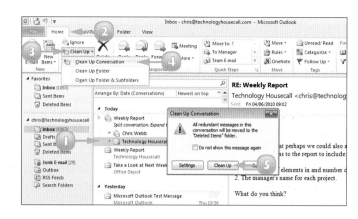

Ignore a Conversation

① Click the conversation you want to ignore.

② Click the **Home** tab.

③ Click the **Ignore** button in the Delete group.

The Ignore Conversation dialog box opens.

④ Click **Ignore Conversation**.

Outlook removes the conversation.

The conversation is placed in the Deleted Items folder.

SCREEN JUNK E-MAIL

Junk e-mail, also called *spam*, is overabundant on the Internet and is likely to find its way onto your computer often. Outlook's Junk E-mail feature enables you to make sure that e-mail from specific Web domains bypasses your Inbox and is instead deposited into the Outlook Junk E-mail folder. You should periodically scan the contents of this folder to ensure that it does not contain any messages you want to read.

You can use rules to determine what Outlook does when you receive a message that meets a specific set of conditions, for example, to send messages from a certain sender into a specific folder.

Create a Message Rule

1. Click the message on which you want to base a rule.

2. Click the **Home** tab.

3. Click **Rules**.

4. Click **Create Rule**.

   The Create Rule dialog box appears.

5. Click to select the conditions that you want to apply.

6. Specify what you want the rule to do when the conditions are met. In this example, select the **Move the item to folder** check box.

7. Click the **Select Folder** button.

   The Rules and Alerts dialog box appears.

8. Click the folder where you want Outlook to move the messages.

9. Click **OK**.

10. Click **OK**.

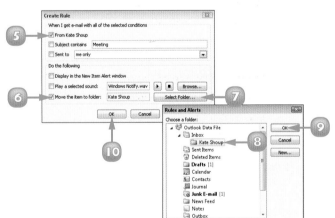

View Junk E-mail Options

1. Click the **Home** tab.

2. Click the **Junk** ▾.

3. Click **Junk E-mail Options**.

   The Junk E-mail Options dialog box appears.

4. Click **OK**.

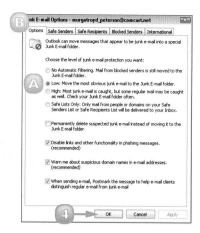

Designate a Message as Junk

1. Click the message.

2. Click the **Home** tab.

3. Click the **Junk** ▾.

4. Click **Block Sender**.

   A message tells you that Outlook has blocked the sender's e-mail address and moved the message to the Junk E-mail folder.

5. Click **OK**.

   Ⓐ You can click one of these options to control the level of junk e-mail filtering that Outlook applies.

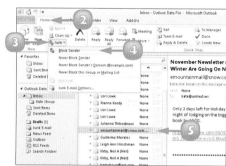

INDEX